AUDIENCE OF ONE

Discovering Ministry to God

JOHAN HEINRICHS

Ordering Information:
Quantity sales. Special discounts are available on quantity purchases.
For details:
mail@johanheinrichs.com

Printed and bound in the USA
Cover design and interior layout | www.pearcreative.ca

ISBN: 978-0-9936542-0-6
ISBN eBook: 978-0-9936542-1-3

*For my kids, Eli, Caitlin and Luke.
May this testimony and message sow into your
identities as priests. You are all called to live
before the Audience of One.*

ACKNOWLEDGMENTS

God has blessed me with a large circle of people who charge one another to live an "Audience of One" lifestyle.

Corrie, for constant support, love and patience. You are amazing, and I could not do any of this without you.

My parents, for sowing so much in so many areas.

My family, who carry the heritage of prayer and Godly values through the ever extending branches of our family tree.

Brian Creary, for being a "priest leading the priests" and calling us to a vision and lifestyle before the Lord.

Joel, for being iron that sharpens iron, year after year. Pine Box.

Tyler, Andrew, Jason and Yvonne, for sowing into my identity as a priest, before I even knew it.

My House of Prayer comrades! Thank you for serving and continuing to serve along side me.

Yvonne Parks, for your great work and mentorship.

Bryan, for your wisdom and input.

Thank you to those who have helped me make sense of my thoughts and story in the editing process.

CONTENTS

FOREWORD

In this book, you are about to discover one of the most important and essential ideas in the Christian faith. In fact, it is one of the most significant ideas in all of life and existence. As grand as this claim is, you will also happily realize that this idea is both easy to understand and within reach. As the very title suggests, there is One who exists outside of time and space and is keenly aware and interested in every detail of your journey. You are called to make Him the focus of your life. He is the audience that your efforts are directed toward and, in the end, nothing other than His response to them really matters.

I have known Johan for many years and can tell you that he is a man of deep devotion to Jesus. He has known for most of his life that he has been called to serve God in a full-time way, and he has sought to live in preparation of this calling because of this. Watching him now as he serves on our staff at Sanctuary House of Prayer, I can see that he is endeavouring to walk out the very ideas he writes about in this book. He understands something that the Lord requires to be central for each of us, and he has written a concise description to help us find it.

There is a transition taking place in the church world wide right now. It is fair to say that many churches have lost their way, and the culture has moved on to a more post-Christian mindset. Jesus fully intends, however, to have his church strong, mature and completely ready for his return at the end of this age. He is stirring people in every stream to feel dissatisfied with the current church expression. He is calling them back to this central reality of the "Audience of One." Once again, God will truly be the centre of everything, and the church will embody this reality as it aligns itself with Him. There are great days ahead. This book is going to help you move in that direction. May He speak to your heart and mind as you read it.

Brian Creary

Director
Sanctuary House of Prayer Missions Base
Winnipeg, Canada

Fellowship with God leads straight to obedience and good works. That is the divine order and it can never be reversed.

-A.W. Tozer

PREFACE

We all understand the subject of this book in theory. We all know and have heard the expression "It's all for Jesus and His glory," yet we consistently go through life in a way that it is easily forgotten or does not really stand at the forefront of our Christian walk. Sadly, it has almost come to the point where it is quoted so often and practised so little that it is becoming Christian jargon, no longer holding any real depth of meaning.

There is an invitation from the Lord to revive our thinking when it comes to bringing glory to Jesus; not to let it be something we just nod our heads to when we hear it, but actually to live it out as the main posture of our heart in life and ministry to God.

My goal is not to be critical, but to be invitational in taking a journey to discovering the treasure of our existence. I wrote this book as a means to boast in my weaknesses, as I have often been guilty of forgetting to give God the glory and to make my life and ministry about His fame.

The Lord put it on my heart to share this testimony and message in the summer of 2012. I never had any dream or inclination to write a book, but writing down the message has been a reminder to myself of its importance and has solidified the message on my heart in a way that I could more confidently articulate it. My hope for this book is that it will be a simple reminder of why we are here and a testimony of how I got to where I am today.

This is my testimony of the Lord's gentle leading, the journey He has taken me on to discovering my true call, the true call of every human. My desire is that this message would go beyond words and jargon. Oh that the glory of God would be the measure of my success! I hope this book will remind us to ask these questions in every life situation: Was I giving glory to Jesus? Did He have all of my heart when I did that? Who was that about, me or Him?

I've ministered in various capacities in my life so far, and when I didn't feel successful I would usually say, "It matters because it's for Jesus." While this is good, I didn't often say or hear it said when I *did* experience success. Of course, the Lord, in His grace and gentle teaching, still blessed what I was doing when my heart was positioned to advance His kingdom and purposes. The issue stemmed from the fact that God and His glory were not always at the forefront of my mind when I served. I always had a picture of the Spirit working through me to do a good work in others, rather than the Lord being magnified and glorified through the work He was doing in me. Thankfully, the Lord knows our weaknesses and will use us anyway.

There are many times I can remember people being impacted by my ministry, times when I have felt the presence of the Lord in what I was doing. I've had opportunities to work with or be in the presence of well-known leaders in the church. It has often ended with the people and the moment coming and going and then I think, *That was nice and even fun . . . now what?*

I grew up with a strong conviction that my ministry would make an impact on thousands upon thousands of people. I've had dreams, prophecies and encounters that all pointed to the importance of the call on my life and the impact it would have, but I was never clear on what that call was. Most often the ministry that I have been involved in or drawn to had to do with music and, more specifically, music in the context of church worship. Even at the age of three I remember closing my bedroom door to play with a tape recorder my parents taught me to use, and I would record myself singing worship songs on cassettes. One of my favourite songs, "David Danced Before the Lord," became significant in my journey to greater intimacy with God as I learned more about David, a man after God's heart.

I have never had the ability in my own strength to make any impact in ministry. I am, and always have been, a weak and broken human just like anyone else. If there was any impact from what I have done in ministry or life, it was the work of the Holy Spirit. The Lord will take our weaknesses and use them for His purposes; in fact, I am convinced that He thoroughly enjoys the process. God sent His Son, who took on our weak frame, to save humanity by humbly dying on a cross, and He enjoyed doing it that way. Isaiah 53:10 says that it "pleased the Lord to bruise Him."

Conversely, He will often take our strengths and use them for humble purposes. This paradox of weakness and strength has been proven in my life, time and time again. The key to it all is how we allow our heart to respond and how we posture ourselves in moments of strength and weakness.

This doesn't end with ministry, of course. What about the mundane things, the everyday chores or pleasures we involve ourselves in? Do we ever stop to consider that the Lord wants them to be for Him, to bring Him glory? We think these things are so mundane that God doesn't even care about them, but He does. When His creation stops to bless His name, there is an explosion of joy that enters His heart. Even though this message has impacted my life significantly, I know I need constant reminders to change my understanding of living the Christian life, even in the little and most mundane things. Paul said it so plainly:

> *Therefore, whether you eat or drink, or whatever you do, do all to the glory of God.*

-1 Corinthians 10:31

Whether we are aware of it or not, there is a God searching the earth for true worshippers who are in love with Him. When He looks down on us from heaven, what is He seeing? Is He seeing people who are captivated by Him and in love? Or is He seeing people who are serving without any connection to His heart?

You could be one of the greatest evangelists, preachers, worship leaders or missionaries, but if you are not deeply connected to the Lord's heart in relationship, it doesn't matter anyway. What does this all have to do with this book? You will find out as I share my story.

It took many years for me to stumble into understanding the importance of ministering out of a connection with the Lord's heart. He has been teaching me and, even to this day, continues to teach me what this means. Hopefully this book will help you enter into this life-changing paradigm of the *Audience of One*.

God's Word says that when we seek the Lord, He comes to His temple. We must check here to see what it is that we who are praying for revival are seeking. We are not seeking fame, miracles, success, ease, full churches, or financial deliverance. These may come. But first and foremost we seek the Lord.

-Leonard Ravenhill

ONE

Empty Rooms & Open Heavens

I was 17 years old and in my 12th grade year at a public high school, longing to be finished. I knew I wanted to be in ministry (whatever that looked like), but learning all the things that the public school system was trying to put in my head was not going to get me there. People often told me that I was a 30 year old trapped in a kid's body. It made it all the more difficult to finish off my graduation year without many friends in the school. It's not that I ever had trouble making friends, but it was a huge school and it was my first year there. Most of my friendships existed within my church community or with my old friends from the small Christian school where I had spent the previous years. The school only went to grade 11, so I was forced to complete my final year in our city's largest public high school. I felt like an outsider.

Every day it was the same thing. Through a haze of cigarette smoke, I would walk down the front path of the school to the front doors. I'd then walk through the over-crowded hallway to my locker, silently repeating to myself how I was an alien, a term that I took from 1 Peter 2:11. I felt like a stranger in a foreign land. At the end of the day, I left as quickly as possible.

It was a much different experience in a public school compared to prior years, which were filled with spiritual growth and where the knowledge of the Word of God permeated every class subject. Here it felt like all the subjects were trying to erase all the things I had learned those previous years. I now found myself in a world among teens who were smoking, taking drugs, craving the latest fashions and partying. Most of them aspired to have nice cars and high paying jobs. Then there was me—I wanted to be a worship leader.

TAKING ADVANTAGE OF MY SITUATION

One redeeming factor of being in this public school was that one of the teachers was an elder at my church (although he did not teach any of my subjects). Halfway through the year, I began leading worship at the Christian youth group that he held at lunch hour once a week. Most of the students who attended were younger than me; I was often the only senior student in the group. I never really developed any friendships there, but I enjoyed the opportunity to practise my worship leading.

Another redeeming factor was my ability to use English class to sing the gospel over my classmates and teacher. I was in the Advanced English course, and the class required two presentations every month: one on a book we read, and one on our community volunteering. Through singing, I found a way that I could connect my presentations to something involving God.

My community volunteering was done in the church serving the poor and playing bass on worship teams. For my presentation, I would usually write a song, somehow relating it to the subject matter. I had a great system going. I was singing and sharing the gospel with my teacher and classmates and, at the same time, getting top marks for it because my teacher was so impressed by my fearlessness.

The book reports were also interesting. We could choose our own book as long as it was level appropriate. I always used the Christian books that my parents had on the shelf at home: books about revival, prophetic encounters, and Biblical studies. My teacher sat me down once and said, "I'm glad you are doing your reports, but I need you to do a different genre, perhaps a fiction book?" I didn't let it stop me; I took a *Christian* fiction book by Frank Peretti and wrote my report on spiritual warfare!

I felt like I was beating the system; it almost became a game and a challenge for me. I remember going into the year saying, "If I can't finish out my education in a Christian school, then I'm going to bring Christ in myself. I'm going to make this a Christian school!"

INNER CITY MINISTRY CENTRE

I grew up as a preacher's kid. When I was 14, my parents decided to take a sabbatical from ministry. They began looking for a new church and found one in the inner city of Winnipeg. The church was what I would describe as a large, very dynamic and diversified church community. The building where we met on Sundays was borrowed, but the church had a secondary building, a former bank, in the inner city called the ministry centre. The ministry centre served as church offices and a place where we would demonstrate the love of Jesus by serving the poor through worship, prayer, food, clothing distribution and relationship.

On weeknights, the church held worship and prayer meetings to intercede for the inner city community and our city in general, contending for a breakthrough. I played bass guitar for some of the worship leaders, which was a good place for me to practise my instrument and fill up my spare time.

Fortunately, the time I spent in the Christian school gave me a lot of extra credits, so the first half of my grade 12 year I was able to take half of the day off. Not being your typical teenager, I rarely slept in past 9am, and I always went to bed at a decent time. When I didn't have to work a shift at the bakery where I was employed part-time, I would frequently go to the ministry centre to play bass or make sandwiches for the street folk. However, I would go more often in the evenings when the focus was on worship and prayer.

Evening meetings were smaller, with less than a dozen people. If there were only a few people in the room, sometimes the leader would take a moment to say a quick prayer and then send those few home, opting not to worship at all. I remember on quite a few occasions dragging my bass and my large, heavy amplifier and speaker out of my tiny white Hyundai hatchback into the building, only to be sent back home because the worship leader didn't show up. At times I was left standing outside because no one answered the door. It was becoming a chore dragging my bass speaker everywhere.

My first instrument was the bass guitar. Although I enjoyed playing it, the greater desire of my heart was to lead corporate worship. I was not a great guitar player, but I was eager to learn the instrument well enough so I could lead worship. During this time, I led worship in a few different house groups throughout the week. Any opportunity I had to learn the skills it took to be a worship leader, I would take. This is what I wanted to do in life. I knew in order for me to lead corporately, I would have to put in a lot of time serving in whatever capacity the church needed me.

My waiting and serving paid off when one of the worship leaders had to cancel, and I was blessed with the opportunity to lead worship for the Monday night meeting at the ministry centre. It was the moment I had been waiting for; I was finally able to pull out my vintage cherry 1983 Ibanez electric guitar and lead worship! I arrived at the front doors, and an associate pastor let me in so I could get ready for the worship and prayer meeting.

After setting up my gear on stage and tuning my guitar, I waited for the people to show up so that the meeting could begin. Seven o'clock rolled around and then ten after, but no one came through the doors. After having put in hours of serving and leading worship in house groups, the moment I had been waiting for—the opportunity to lead corporate worship in the church arrived. Lo and behold, no one showed up. You can imagine my disappointment.

I looked down from the stage at the pastor and, with a hint of disappointment in my voice, said, "So, I guess we're cancelling tonight, huh?" Seemingly ignoring my suggestion she responded, "Just go for it." I chuckled, thinking she was joking, but then all of a sudden I felt uncomfortable and confused, realizing she was not being facetious.

Now, I've been in front of crowds before playing bass, singing and speaking. I can handle larger groups without many nerves. Most people who perform regularly in a large group setting will tell you that it is much easier than in a small group. What I wasn't prepared for was having only one person in the room, watching my every move and singing to my set. The intimacy and smallness of the situation was very uncomfortable. I couldn't say no since this was finally the opportunity I had been waiting for, and yet the pastor was the one person I would be leading in worship!

Ever have one of those dreams where you go to school or are in front of a class or group of people, and then realize you're in your underwear because you forgot to put on clothes? This was how I felt in that moment. I felt inadequate, insecure and unprepared.

Nervously, I swallowed the ball sitting in my throat and, with sweaty palms and shaky hands, I adjusted my song sheets in order on the music stand. I remember a few sheets floating to the ground as I did so. I shut off the world around me by closing my eyes. I started to play my guitar and sing, trying to find a happy place in my head to keep me from the reality of this seemingly precarious situation.

It was strange for the first little bit; I stole a glance, squinting with one eye to see if anyone else had come in since the song started. Nope, still just me, the pastor and an empty, dark room. However, the pastor was not staring at me blankly and unengaged as I had envisioned. There she was in front of me five feet from the stage, hands outstretched, singing and worshipping like she would if there was a band and a room full of people.

All of a sudden, something washed over me as I stood there singing. I felt she had something I didn't have—and I wanted it! The pastor had clearly come prepared to commune with the Holy Spirit and to worship the living God. I came prepared to lead a group of people and share the anointed gift I thought I possessed to further my agenda of leading corporate worship. There in that moment, I felt a wrestle in my spirit concerning the intention of my heart and the vision for my life. I was left with a decision to make: do I keep singing just to get through the night? Or do I enter into worship before the God I have set my life to love and serve?

I resolved to shift my focus, to stand and sing to God rather than lead my pastor in worship. I imagined myself in my room at home, singing like I would normally do. It was then that I felt the pressure lift, and it was replaced by the pleasure and the presence of the Lord on my heart. Worshipping on that stage in that empty room actually made sense to me. I was unable to define it and, therefore, it was not yet my pursuit as a lifestyle, but it felt right in that moment.

I still felt my future destiny was to lead hundreds of people, but for now this was a good way to learn my skill—in an empty room, singing to God. I did not fully grasp what it meant to minister before the Audience of One, but I got a taste of it. I would have a similar experience later on in life where it would finally click.

CLICK

Several years later, it started to make sense to me during one late evening set in the very beginning stages of Sanctuary House of Prayer, my current church community. People shuffled out of the little building we were using after a long day of hard work in the House of Prayer. We had just finished a worship and intercession set, and this was often the time the majority of the people went home because the hour was late. The five or six of us scheduled to lead the next worship set walked up to the stage only to realize that everyone who did not leave was now on the stage. It was just us and a room full of empty brown chairs. We were left with a big question: do we just go home because no one is here? It was late after all, and we were all a little tired. Or do we finish up the day and keep worshipping? It was going to be a Worship with the Word set, a time to declare and learn Scripture by singing it right out of the passage. Were we going to sing to an empty room? We were forced to ask ourselves why we were there. Was it simply to grow a prayer movement in our city? Or was our primary objective to bring glory and worship to Jesus?

I don't know who made the final decision, but we decided to go through with the full, hour-long set. We dimmed the lights in the sanctuary with just enough light to see our song sheets, simply because we enjoyed the atmosphere—and the empty brown chairs didn't exactly need any light. We started to worship. We let our voices fill that empty building and, as the set progressed, we began to feel the pleasure of the Lord over us. The hour flew by with little effort and when it ended, we didn't want to leave.

The group singing on stage that night fell in love with empty prayer rooms. We had many more empty prayer rooms after that evening, and we cherished every opportunity we had thereafter to sing to an empty room, or rather, to God alone. I can recall the days when people decided to stay for those late sets, and we would almost wish they would go home! Although I am a big advocate for having a large group sing together, it was a special season of posturing our hearts and figuring out why we were there to sing in the first place.

Nowadays, empty prayer rooms are harder to come by, but the Lord planted something within our hearts that would become a treasure and prepare us for a lifestyle of worship, prayer and ministry to the Lord. Though we didn't coin the phrase Audience of One, it became alive in our hearts and part of our culture and language in the prayer room. The Audience of One paradigm has defined my life's pursuit of ministry and the ministry He has called me to do—ministry to the Lord Himself.

You are worthy of all glory, honour and praise. Whether it's a building full of people or just me in an empty room, You are deserving of every song, prayer and glance in Your direction. Give me joy in the secret place.

I have one passion. It is He, only He.

-Count Zinzendorf

TWO

DEFINITIONS & THE FIRST COMMANDMENT

The Audience of One paradigm is simply defined as ministry to the Lord. It means to minister to God and worship Him exclusively in your heart for the sole purpose of giving Him glory. It is worship to Him alone because He alone is worthy. It's worship He deserves and requires from every person with nothing expected in return, where everything we do is for His pleasure, before His feet and before His throne. It mirrors the worship that is constantly taking place in heaven.

To best paint a picture of what the Audience of One paradigm means, we need to turn to Revelation 4. Everything described in this passage points to the One on the throne. When we read it we may think that because there is so much happening, it could distract from the One on the throne, but it is quite the opposite.

Everything around His throne describes or reveals something about God and His character. Those things are there because He wants them to be. God enjoys the things He put around His throne. God will not share glory with another; therefore, He chose the activity that is happening around His throne to reveal something about Himself. There is no denying that all eyes in heaven are on Him.

Many Christians are familiar with Revelation 4; however, it is not something we can skip over just because we've read it countless times before. There is endless fascination and revelation waiting to be derived from this passage!

The moment we get bored reading Revelation 4 is the moment we need to stop everything and ask God for a renewed revelation of His Son and a longing for eternity.

> *After these things I looked, and behold, a door standing open in heaven. And the first voice which I heard was like a trumpet speaking with me, saying, "Come up here, and I will show you things which must take place after this." Immediately I was in the Spirit; and **behold, a throne** set in heaven, and **One sat on the throne**. And **He who sat there** was like a jasper and a sardius stone in appearance; and there was a rainbow **around the throne**, in appearance like an emerald. Around the throne were twenty-four thrones, and on the thrones I saw twenty-four elders sitting, clothed in white robes; and they had crowns of gold on their heads. And **from the throne** proceeded lightnings, thunderings, and voices. Seven lamps of fire were burning **before the throne**, which are the seven Spirits of God.*

Before the throne there was a sea of glass, like crystal. And in the midst of the throne, and around the throne, were four living creatures full of eyes in front and in back. The first living creature was like a lion, the second living creature like a calf, the third living creature had a face like a man, and the fourth living creature was like a flying eagle. The four living creatures, each having six wings, were full of eyes around and within. And they do not rest day or night, saying:

> **"Holy, holy, holy, Lord God Almighty,**
> **Who was and is and is to come!"**

*Whenever the living creatures give glory and honour and thanks to Him who sits **on the throne**, who lives forever and ever, the twenty-four elders fall down before Him **who sits on the throne** and worship Him who lives forever and ever, and cast their crowns **before the throne, saying:***

> *"You are worthy, O Lord, To receive glory*
> *and honour and power;*
> *For You created all things, And by Your will*
> *they exist and were created."*

-Revelation 4 (emphasis mine)

The throne is mentioned several times in this chapter. In his vision, it seems clear to me that John couldn't take his eyes off of the throne. Everything depicted in this passage is described in its proximity to the throne. God's throne is the centrepiece of heaven and of the universe; everything created in the universe was created from that same throne and is made to bring glory to the One sitting there.

When we read it, the description of the throne room in heaven seems outrageous. Still, we need to press through our unbelief and try to imagine it. Our imagination is a treasure given to us by God and a tool to help us connect with His beauty.

Creativity in all of humanity comes from the imagination. I believe God gave us imagination not only for creativity but also for help with eternal perspectives. He wants to purify our imagination through beholding His beauty.

I believe the most important thing that should come to mind when we set our life goals and vision is where they put *us* in proximity to His throne. Are our goals and activities taking us further away from His throne, or are they drawing us closer to His presence and before His throne in worship? Revelation 4 is a perfect picture of what it looks like to worship the Audience of One. It is the very essence of what it means to worship in spirit and in truth.

John's vision begins with a voice saying, "Come up here, and I will show you things which must take place after this." The first thing we see in this vision is the worship of heaven. We see a Kingdom obsessed with their King, a prayer room full of activity focused on giving Him all glory and honour, and a place energized by how completely transcendent He is in glory, beauty and majesty. But why is the throne room scene at the beginning of the vision?

God wants us to know that the activity of worship is what we were made for and its importance in how we relate to Him. He also knows we need a revelation of true worship in order to come victoriously through the culmination of all other events in Revelation.

In the final juncture of this age, God will have people who are lovesick worshippers. He will be our only audience and He will receive all the love, adoration and glory that is due His name. The very definition of the word *holy* tells us that God is the only audience in heaven. It means to stand alone or to be completely on another level apart from anything else, and that is exactly what He is.

When trying to convey the Audience of One message, I find it is important to know this is not a new philosophy, a new gimmick or the next trendy thing. It is simply language we can use to help us return to true worship. It's the alignment of our hearts with the Lord's heart concerning His intention to bring to Himself all the glory that is due His name. He is worthy of it all and will not share it with another.

> *For My own sake, for My own sake, I will do it; For how should My name be profaned? And I will not give My glory to another.*
>
> -Isaiah 48:11

> *I am the Lord, that is My name; And My glory I will not give to another, Nor My praise to carved images.*
>
> -Isaiah 42:8

THE FIRST AND THE GREATEST COMMANDMENT

One of the major verses pertaining to this theme of focused worship is Jesus' first and greatest commandment:

> *Jesus said to him, "You shall love the Lord your God with all your heart, with all your soul, and with all your mind."*
>
> -Matthew 22:37

Jesus gave this commandment not so that we would have another important rule to follow, but out of affectionate longing in His heart to have intimacy with His bride. Those who practise an Audience of One lifestyle are people who have entered into deep revelation of the first and greatest commandment that Jesus gave to us. It's not just a conscious decision to give Him glory; it's about giving glory to God out of a natural expression of a heart that has caught a glimpse of Him, a heart that is so lovesick for Him that nothing else will do but to pour out all its love, affection and attention on Him alone.

We can't even begin to scratch the surface of loving God with all our heart, soul and mind, but at least we know where it is going. The bar has been set and we have an end goal.

Giving Him all that we are and have is not a one-off moment where we can say, "There Lord, it's yours. I did it!" Giving Him our heart, soul and mind is a lifetime process that requires difficult, heart level decisions day after day and hour after hour. It is something that we mature in and hopefully get better at through years of pouring out our lives at His feet. Thankfully, He helps us and teaches us along the way.

When we take time to meditate on this commandment, we may find it helpful to approach it as we would a wedding ceremony. Our worship is like the tender moment of sharing vows. We are staring into the eyes of our Beloved and telling Him we will love Him with all we are and have. It is like the precious moment when we are committing our life, energy and heart to the one we love. Repeating His word back to Him in worship and prayer is like reciting the marriage vows we have prepared. It becomes part of our story, it becomes real in our hearts, and we develop a resolve to see our vows through to the end. We are entering into a deep and untainted marriage relationship where we desire to give all we have to the One we love.

I believe we are entering a time like no other. As we approach the day of His return, God is preparing a wedding and would have us prepare as His bride. Revelation 19 talks about the wedding supper of the Lamb, and the bride is making herself ready. This changes our whole perception of Jesus, making Him a lot more involved and intimate than what we give Him credit for.

When we come to the understanding that He views us as His bride, it also changes the way we approach Him. It gives us confidence to draw near to Him, knowing that He is desiring to see and hear us. In Song of Solomon 2, He beckons:

> *"Oh my dove, in the clefts of the rock, in the secret places of the cliff, let me see your face, let me hear your voice; For your voice is sweet and your face is lovely."*

Our bridegroom jealously desires all of our attention and affection.

He could have called us servants, but as we read in John 15:15, we are not called servants, but rather His friends. It's all about relationship, a relationship where there is a reciprocal exchange of pleasure and adoration.

Many Christians are disconnected servants who base their faith on works. We may be productive and successful in ministry, but if we serve out of obligation and not relationship, it doesn't matter. We can work for Him, prophesy in His name, and teach the next generation about Him, but in the end we need to know His heart.

> *Not everyone who says to Me, 'Lord, Lord,' shall enter the kingdom of heaven, but he who does the will of My*

Father in heaven. Many will say to Me in that day, 'Lord, Lord, have we not prophesied in Your name, cast out demons in Your name, and done many wonders in Your name?' And then I will declare to them, 'I never knew you; depart from Me, you who practise lawlessness!'

-Matthew 7:21-23

ON EARTH AS IT IS IN HEAVEN

"Your kingdom come.
Your will be done
On earth as it is in heaven."

-Matthew 6:10

Earlier we read Revelation 4 with the descriptions of the throne room. As mentioned, Revelation 4 paints the best picture of what it means to be before the Lord, the Audience of One. God is at the centre of all worship and activity, and everything around Him is bringing attention to His beauty and revealing His character. This is not a figurative picture nor is it something that is meant to exclude us. God wants the worship and activity that is happening around His throne to be manifest the same way on the earth: "Your kingdom come, Your will be done on earth as it is in heaven."

If Jesus tells us to pray something, it must be important to Him. Jesus gave this prayer to us so that it would become a longing of our hearts. He said, "Pray this way," because this is a prayer He intends to bring to fruition. This simple prayer (Your kingdom come . . .) can be used as a tool to posture our hearts before the Lord in an Audience of One lifestyle.

Lord, let Your kingdom come and Your will be done here as it is in heaven. Jesus, show me what the elders are seeing. What is captivating them? What sustains their resolve to bring You glory hour after hour? What is it that makes You so beautiful? Give me a deeper revelation of who You are.

In prayer it is better to have a heart
without words than words without a heart.

-John Bunyan

THREE

LANGUAGE BARRIERS & HEART INTERIORS

In order to better grasp what the Audience of One paradigm means, we need help. We need a revelation from the Holy Spirit to teach us about the character of Jesus, to reveal Jesus to our hearts and to fascinate us.

I've heard it said many times that when performing or stepping out in front of a group, you need to "know your audience." It was a special moment when I heard this phrase one day and related it to worship unto God. Fortunately, we have the Holy Spirit who has done all the research for us and helps us to "know our audience." 1 Corinthians 2:10 tells us that the Spirit searches the deep things of God. The same Spirit that searches the deep things reveals those same things to us.

The Holy Spirit is our helper, but do we ever stop to think about what He is there to help us with? We tend to make it about ourselves; He is helping us not to sin, He convicts us of our sin, and He gives us direction and helps us to live holy lives. While these are most definitely true and good, the Spirit helping to make us holy is not about us. It's about God having people holy enough to draw close to Him and offer true worship.

Romans 12:1 tells us that it is true and proper worship to offer our bodies as a living sacrifice, holy and pleasing to God. The Holy Spirit is all about worshipping and glorifying the Son. His primary objective is to reveal Jesus to our hearts and declare the same things to us that God did when His Spirit was sent like a dove.

And the Holy Spirit descended in bodily form like a dove upon Him, and a voice came from heaven which said, "You are My beloved Son; in You I am well pleased."

-Luke 3:22

When the Holy Spirit descended at Jesus' baptism, three things happened:

1. God declared Jesus to be His divine Son (You are my Son).

2. God proclaimed His love for the Son (My beloved Son).

3. God validated Jesus' ministry, which was His words and works (with You I am well pleased).

The Holy Spirit hasn't changed; He continues to declare these things to our hearts as He dwells within us. He desires and invites us to partner with Him, declaring who Jesus is in His divinity, declaring love and affection for Him, and declaring with revelation all His marvellous works and teachings. This is worshipping in truth.

He [the Holy Spirit] will glorify Me, for He will take of what is Mine and declare it to you.

-John 16:14

Revealing Jesus is what the Holy Spirit does and continues to do. In revealing the Son to us, He becomes the object of our devotion, affection and attention. He brings us into unity and agreement with Him by bringing glory to Jesus. If the Holy Spirit is all about the Audience of One lifestyle, I want to be found in full agreement with Him.

But when the Helper comes, whom I shall send to you from the Father, the Spirit of truth who proceeds from the Father, He will testify of Me.

-John 15:26

But the Helper, the Holy Spirit, whom the Father will send in My name, He will teach you all things, and bring to your remembrance all things that I said to you.

-John 14:26

LEARNING TO WORSHIP

In the years before my experience leading worship at the ministry centre, I was involved in a few of the house groups in our church. Since I couldn't exactly lead worship with the bass, I had to learn how to play the guitar. I got myself an acoustic guitar and became an eager learner. My dad helped me learn the basic chords and got me going.

On Sundays, I would sit near the front of the church so I could watch the worship leader's hands as they played the chords, and then I would try them myself when I got home. I played bass on a few different worship teams, so not only was I able to observe a few guitar players close up, but I was also able to get song sheets and charts to bring home and practise on my own.

I remember the exciting day I was given the church's coil-bound song booklet for worship leaders because it seemed like an elusive tool to get at the time; it felt like I was handed my graduation papers, and I thought, *Now I can start my worship leader internship.*

I started picking up a lot of little tricks, and I eventually got good enough that I could play alongside others while they were leading. I had the ability to play by ear because of my experience playing bass and being immersed in church music my whole life. This helped me play guitar in house groups when they didn't have charts for me.

Fortunately, one of the house groups I was going to (a teen/college group) had a few guitar players. They asked if I played and let me bring my guitar to strum along. I enjoyed playing, but I really wanted to start leading.

After many months of playing guitar beside others while they led, the leaders finally asked me if I would like to lead a song. Since I had learned a few songs by heart, I was excited about the opportunity. Everyone in the group was always so positive and encouraging to one another. They knew there were some up-and-coming leaders, and they were all supportive and excited when someone would demonstrate their gifts who had not done so before.

When the day came for me to lead, I had my song prepared and ready. The main worship leader in the house group got started with a song or two, and then he looked in my direction and gave me a nod when it was time to play my song. This was pretty much the first time anybody in our community heard me lead. I chose a song that they often sang at the house group so it would be familiar and they could join in and help me along. It seemed to go well; everybody engaged in worship, and a few others who played guitar backed me up, so it made it easy. I got a lot of helpful feedback that encouraged me and kept me wanting to lead more often.

I don't know if word got around that I could lead worship or if it was simply the Lord providing more opportunities, but after leading at this house group a few times, I was asked to do one song at another house group that I was attending.

The house group leaders (who were married) were both awesome worship leaders whom I deeply admired. I always found that I could talk to them whenever I needed encouragement. They were welcoming when I came to the church and always willing to provide opportunities for a young worship leader-in-training. Because they were fairly young, it was easy to connect with them. They told me some great stories about their development as worship leaders and how they became a couple in that season. We quickly became great friends.

I was a little more nervous to lead at this house group simply because of the profound respect I had for the leaders. Not only that, the other members of this house group were all adults older than me, whereas the other house groups I was attending primarily consisted of young people. Since I was not one to pass up this kind of opportunity, I came prepared with my song. It started off as a very similar experience as last time. The main leader played a few songs while I played guitar. In fact, I am fairly certain I even played the same song that I did at the other house group. The people in the room all sang along, so that made things a whole lot easier than I was expecting. I thought it went well, although it felt very mechanical and I was evaluating myself based on the fact that I didn't make any mistakes.

After the house group was over, I stuck around for a few minutes, hoping to get some feedback. Sure enough, the house group leader approached me. I thought, *Here comes the follow up*, but secretly I hoped he would see something that went beyond my leading. Perhaps he would give me a prophetic word, or maybe he would see something concerning my future destiny as a worship leader. This was both a nervous and exciting moment for me.

He said, "Dude, can I talk with you for a minute? Great job leading that song! Your guitar playing is really coming along. You have great timing and that song really suits you. In fact, I think I'd like you to lead a whole set here some time, and we'll see where it goes." *So far so good*, I thought. He continued, "Although, I feel there is something missing . . . "

The nerves that had diminished because of his high praise immediately came back to me. He asked me, "Do you speak in tongues regularly?"

I responded, "Yes, but not too often . . . I started when I was about eight."

"Good," he said. "Now how about *singing* in tongues or singing in the Spirit?"

"I don't . . . I haven't really tried anything like that," I replied apprehensively. And then I went on the defensive and made a quick excuse: "I'm still learning to lead worship songs. I don't want to get too complicated."

He then said something that would plant a seed in my heart and stir something within the depths of my soul: "I think the Lord has something for you there. I think you should try it. Next time you lead, why don't you give it a try?"

All I could think to say at this point was, "Uh . . . okay."

I can honestly say I came home from that evening upset. It was hard enough for me to lead worship in front of all these adults, and now he wanted me not only to speak in tongues (which I did not do on a regular basis) but also to sing in the Spirit while leading a worship set that I am trying to avoid making mistakes on? This was supposed to be encouraging? This was supposed to be the advice that was going to take me to the next level as a worship leader? This was the prophetic word that was going to speak into my destiny as a worship leader? I did not appreciate or understand the simple answer to all those questions in my head at the time, but the answer was 'yes.'

In my offence and insecurity, I remember avoiding my guitar for a few days while I let the house group leader's words settle in my heart. When I finally decided to play my guitar again, I pulled out my songbook and thumbed through it. I was still disheartened and did not really feel like playing anything, but since I would have to lead soon, I knew I had better get it over with and practise. I also knew I was expected to sing in tongues during my next set at that specific house group.

So, in my practice time I sang through a simple song. When I got to the end, I just kept on the same chord progression. I started speaking in tongues over top of the music. Sure enough, I made mistakes in my playing while I did this. I could not for the life of me connect a melody from my guitar to what came out of my mouth. I started to get frustrated with my voice, my instrument and speaking in tongues in general. This was not what I had signed up for!

In that moment, I felt the Lord whisper to me in my spirit, "Just lift up your voice to *Me*." I shut off all the mechanics and distractions that were getting in my way. I didn't worry about my mistakes. I decided to start lifting up my voice to God, no matter what came out.

It was awkward at first; it was not easy to sing a melody when there were no English words to sing. I started by singing short and simple phrases and adding tongues in between. It was very disjointed and not as free flowing as one would want when singing in the Spirit, but I kept at it and finally grabbed a melody. It was simple and short enough that it flowed well, and I did not make too many mistakes. It was also a melody that was stirring something within my heart.

I was beginning to feel something different inside than when I would lead songs from a book. I didn't have the language to describe it then, but now I would describe it as communing with the Holy Spirit. Even though my singing in the Spirit was limited to a simple melodic phrase, it was a seed that would eventually define my worship leading experience.

Weeks later I ended up leading a full set at the same house group. At the tail end of a song, I played the same melody and sang the same melodic phrase I had practised and that I hoped was actually singing in the Spirit. It probably lasted a whole ten seconds, but it was a start.

Now I encourage all new worship leaders by saying, "Just try it, just start doing it at home. It's not easy at first, it takes practice, but you just gotta start doing it." In the years following, the same house group leaders continued to sow into me. Through their teaching gift, I learned how to commune with the Holy Spirit. I am so thankful for that season when the Lord put me under their leadership.

SINGING IN THE SPIRIT

I am by no means an expert on singing in the Spirit, but I have heard some amazing teachings on it, and I can draw from my few experiences and share bits of revelation that I have picked up along the way.

First of all, I have found that singing in the Spirit has been essential in devoting my life to the Audience of One lifestyle. I use it at home as well as on stage, and it has proven to be beneficial beyond measure time and time again.

Often when approaching your time before God, it's hard to know where to begin. A cold start with a prayer and not really feeling the presence of the Lord can quickly lead to boredom and distraction. Though this won't always be the case, you will find it is difficult to sustain over time, and you may feel like quitting.

Another way to start your prayer time is to simply read Scripture, hoping some revelation opens up for you and leads to a successful conversation with God. While prayer and Scripture reading can lead to powerful devotional times with the Lord, I have found singing to be the most effectual way to initially approach God in your devotional prayer time because it touches the heart in a greater measure than the other methods. In Scripture we are exhorted to:

> *Serve the Lord with gladness;*
> *Come before His presence with singing.*

-Psalm 100:2

So, what do you sing? I encourage you to begin with singing Scripture. I regularly combine singing Scripture and singing in the Spirit or tongues. Quite often this opens up a door into the Lord's presence and profound revelation of His Word. As you step out, you will find your closet prayer time becoming a joy as you begin to grow deeper in love and communion with the Holy Spirit.

If you are not actively speaking in tongues, just keep asking for it. And in the meantime, lift up your voice and make melody in your heart to the Lord (Ephesians 5:19). Give Him the pleasure of hearing your voice.

When you sing in the Spirit or vocalize from your heart, it brings your thoughts, distractions and emotions under the submission and influence of the Holy Spirit. While it is still valuable and biblical to worship with all your mind, the Holy Spirit helps you to worship with all three: heart, soul *and* mind. When all three are engaged with the Spirit, it causes true worship to arise. When you sing in the Spirit, you're not thinking about what you are saying; you're expressing the language and singing the song that is in your heart. As you press into Him, you will begin to experience *God's* emotions, His thoughts and feelings on your heart. His song will become your song. It's like a song within you that you and the Lord start singing to one another.

The Lord your God in your midst,
The Mighty One, will save;
He will rejoice over you with gladness,
He will quiet you with His love,
He will rejoice over you with singing.

-Zephaniah 3:17

In this dialogue of song, we will often find ourselves in the presence of the Lord. Singing is the activity that is happening in heaven. Music and singing stirs and magnifies our emotions. And because we have been singing, it has a greater impact on our hearts. Singing is the universal language of the heart. David says in Psalm 108, "I will sing and make music with all my soul." This is the depth of song we can enter into with God, where it comes from the deepest part of us—our very souls. The soul is the place where song touches our whole being, our emotions and desires. Song has a profound effect on us whether we know it or not.

CORPORATE BENEFITS

There is so much value in the bride of Christ coming together to sing with one voice. I know as a worship leader that it is almost impossible to get a whole room engaged at once. People come with their own thoughts, moods and distractions. They might not connect with the worship songs, worship leader or style of the music, and there is little a worship leader can do about that. My goal of getting the whole room engaged was abandoned after years of leading corporate sets and realizing that I can't have a whole room engaged at once apart from the Holy Spirit.

People come from all walks of life and situations. There is no way that I can formulate a worship set so that everyone is happy all of the time. I can't know what is happening on the inside; only God knows. Over the years I've had people approach me who seemed like they were checked out the whole time, only to tell me they were really impacted during worship. Who knows how the Lord works at the heart level?

In our house of prayer community, the culture of focusing on God rather than people has changed the way we lead worship. We purposefully make the decision not to try to guide the room. Instead, we aim to create a worshipful atmosphere that produces on-ramps for people to engage their hearts.

When worship becomes a feeling or experience rather than an encounter with the Lord, it is no longer about ministering to His heart. If the Holy Spirit is active in our hearts, we should not need a worship leader to keep us fascinated with God. Obviously this model of corporate worship is not exclusive to the house of prayer, but I can only speak from my experience that it is a great incubator for producing an Audience of One people.

How do we stir up fascination in our prayer lives so that it translates in our corporate worship? We can't. Only God can do this. We can't even love God apart from Him helping us. We love Him because He first loved us. What we *can* do is posture ourselves in the place that allows Him to reveal Himself. We can put ourselves before His throne at His feet, to wait and listen and allow Him to draw us closer. We can rend our hearts.

When we sing in the Spirit during corporate worship, it provides an open door for us to remove barriers that prevent us from worshipping freely. It takes away the words and specific melodies modelled by the worship leader and provides us with an opportunity to sing our own melody or harmony to the Lord without worrying about words to get there. When we lift up our voices in free melody or sing in the Spirit, we are all given a chance to connect with the Lord and to experience God's emotions in our own hearts.

At the same time, we are connecting with God's heart with other believers in unity. It's so enjoyable to go there together; and yet, simultaneously, we connect with the Lord on an individual level. Even if it is simply singing "la la la," it will engage the heart more than if we just choose to listen to what is happening in the room.

This, of course, largely depends on the church community and if speaking in tongues is something they utilize and value. I believe the Lord is eventually going to have His way in this area in every church on the earth. If your community does not currently value speaking in tongues or singing in the Spirit, there is an invitation for you to contend in prayer for the Lord's heart in it for your church. It's also an opportunity to seek His heart for your personal prayer language. The Lord loves and will answer this prayer.

In our house of prayer community, our worship leaders have discovered that singing in the Spirit is one of the most important things we do during the course of our one hour sets. Singing in the Spirit takes the mind, disconnect and performance out of worship leading. In any other scenario, I could easily lead a set of five songs and often not pay any attention to what I am singing or not connect with the songs and simply do my best to lead the room. But when I sing in the Spirit, there are no words to think about. I am just singing melodies to the Lord and not leading the room in a way that I want them to sing, but rather going right for communion with the Spirit living within me.

> *. . .speaking to one another in psalms and hymns and spiritual songs, singing and making melody in your heart to the Lord.*
>
> -Ephesians 5:19

In my experience, singing in the Spirit has proven to be more valuable and precious than the songs themselves. Whenever I ask worship team members where in the set they feel the presence of the Lord or where their heart connects with Him, most often they say it is when they sing in the Spirit.

The house group worship leader who exhorted me to start singing in the Spirit spoke into my life with little knowledge that 15 years later it would be the treasure of my life and essential in the ministry that I would be involved in for years to come. There is no question that it has become my stream of refreshing and has sustained me as a worship leader, as well as helped me keep the Lord in the centre of my attention as my only audience in worship.

JUST SING

Singing in its simplest form is so valuable to the Lord. There are nuances to each individual's voice that make it different from anyone else. There were times when I did not enjoy the sound of my voice. I would get frustrated when I heard someone else sing. I often became jealous and asked the Lord why I couldn't have a voice like theirs.

The Lord spoke to me in my frustration. He said, "You are the only person in all of history and created order that can offer *your* voice. If you don't sing to Me, you are depriving Me of pleasure, of something that I long to hear." When I heard this, it gripped my heart, and I exploded into tears and repented.

It was settled for me on that day. I assure you, no matter how good or bad you think you sound, He loves the sound of your voice, and you need to offer it to Him.

> *"O my dove, in the clefts of the rock,*
> *In the secret places of the cliff,*
> *Let me see your face,*
> *Let me hear your voice;*
> *For your voice is sweet,*
> *And your face is lovely."*

-Song of Solomon 2:14

THE KIND OF WORSHIP THE FATHER SEEKS

> *For the eyes of the Lord run to and fro throughout the whole earth, to show Himself strong on behalf of those whose heart is loyal to Him . . .*

-2 Chronicles 16:9

God seeks worshippers. The God who has everything is searching for something—something we can give—that He cannot have apart from us. It is our voluntary worship and love. He could command worship; He could make rocks cry out. He chose to do it differently, to make worship voluntary and have it come from a heart of desire. Voluntary worship requires a human heart with a free will. This is the very essence of creation and the reason for our existence.

> *"Or who has first given to Him*
> *And it shall be repaid to him?"*
> *For of Him and through Him and to Him are all things,*
> *to whom be glory forever. Amen.*

-Romans 11:35-36

Though voluntary worship is the only thing God cannot have apart from us, we need to understand that He doesn't actually need it. It does not in any way augment His worthiness or glory, but the Lord knows that this is where we will find our deepest joy and pleasure.

We receive the benefits of eternal rewards in heaven as a result of our voluntary love toward Him. There is no shortage of motivation to give Him our hearts. He wants *all* of our hearts. He is a jealous husband and desires voluntary love for Him only. He searches the whole earth to find it, to find true worshippers that are loyal to His heart.

> *"But the hour is coming, and now is, when the true*
> *worshippers will worship the Father in spirit and truth;*
> *for the Father is seeking such to worship Him. God is*
> *Spirit, and those who worship Him must worship*
> *in spirit and truth."*

-John 4:23-24

We could spend a long time trying to figure out what it means to worship in spirit and in truth, and I think this is a lifelong journey we would take with the Lord. That being said, the above passage has a few things that should make our ears perk up. First of all, "the hour is coming and now is". We get a strange quote from Jesus here, indicating now and not yet. I believe that Jesus declared this as the start of a process. The King has arrived and is establishing a kingdom of worship, and the process starts now.

Jesus is establishing the work of His kingdom on the earth. This includes the work of the heart and establishing true worship on earth as it is in heaven. It all culminates in a time when there will be true worshippers in every corner of the earth. In fact, we will be a kingdom of worshippers and priests (1 Peter 2:9, Revelation 1:6) who declare His praises and who He is. He will have people who will minister to His heart.

This is worship that goes beyond what happens in a church, temple or any religious ceremony. This is the work of the Holy Spirit inside us that is turned into worship when we voluntarily agree with Him in His declaration of Jesus. In the process, there will be reciprocal exchange of communion.

". . . the Father is seeking such to worship Him." Nowhere does this passage or any other Scripture say that He is seeking worship from a cold, disconnected heart. Worship is not true worship if it is contrived out of a religious spirit or obligation.

True worship is a response to awe and love; it comes from a lovesick heart and relationship with a God who desires us. The fact that this verse uses the word *Father* tells us that He desires worship out of relationship. The Audience of One lifestyle and true worship cannot be separated from one another.

If we worship with a disconnected heart, our worship is in vain. 1 Corinthians 13 tells us that without love we become sounding brass or a clanging cymbal. In Matthew, Jesus, in speaking about the Pharisees, reiterated what Isaiah said:

" 'These people draw near to Me with their mouth,
And honour Me with their lips,
But their heart is far from Me. And in vain they worship
Me, Teaching as doctrines the commandments of men.' "

-Matthew 15:8-9

So let it be the cry of our hearts, that when He searches the earth to find worshippers, He would find us. When His eyes look down from heaven, He would find our eyes looking up at Him. As He speaks and sings over us, He would find people speaking and singing His Word back to Him, engaged and connected at a heart level . . . singing in the Spirit, and singing with understanding, the truth of His Word that the Holy Spirit is whispering to us. He desires worship and the praise of His glory to flow from every heart, and in this He wants to be our only audience.

Lord, I thank You that You love my voice and that You move at the sound of it. Thank You that You allow this humble creature to move Your heart. Let it be a pure and pleasing fragrance that rises from my heart to Yours. Oh, that You would continually give me new prayer language to bless Your heart! Teach me what it means to worship in spirit and in truth.

We must never rest until
everything inside us worships God.

-A.W. Tozer

FOUR

TREES & SHEEP

1998 was one of the most influential years of my life. I was 15 and in a Christian school at the time. A student teacher named Tyler, who also happened to be a member of the church I was attending, came to my school to do his practicum.

Tyler was a worship leader with an evangelistic heart, qualities that were appealing to a group of young Christians hungry and eager to do things for God. He inspired us to go even further in our ministry pursuits. He took us under his wing and, instead of going out and playing sports at lunch hour, we would go to the gym stage and play worship music. He saw our potential and poured into us.

Tyler was one of the first living, breathing revivalists whom I knew on a personal level. He invited a few of us to campus prayer meetings at the University of Winnipeg. We watched in awe as the university students, full of zeal for God, quoted the great men of God and the revivalists who shaped the modern day church—Tozer, Finney, Whitfield, Ravenhill, Spurgeon and the Wesley brothers—and prayed over our city, asking for revival to come. It stirred our faith. It was like digging ancient wells of revival the Lord poured out a long time ago and anticipating that He would do the same thing today. Tyler encouraged us to pray with the group. We felt like we belonged in those prayer meetings even though we were a few young teenagers among a bunch of university students.

After one of the prayer meetings, we were invited to a popular tobogganing hill in our city to continue the prayer meeting and preach the word of God. My friends and I thought it was a bit weird, but we went anyway. The students explained that they had started a group of intercessors and street evangelists called the Midnight Martyrs. The name was likely derived from the fact that they would often read stories from *Foxe's Book of Martyrs* for inspiration and that the meetings were held late at night.

Pacing back and forth from the heights on the hill and stretching out our hands toward the city, we took turns praying and asking for revival to come. I wanted to do this every night; it was invigorating, and it felt like we were shifting things in the spiritual atmosphere over our city. I was sure revival would break out because of our activity that night. These were the coolest group of guys I had ever met, and I was immediately drawn to their hunger and lifestyle of prayer and revival. We all left encouraged and looked forward to the next Midnight Martyrs prayer meeting.

AUDIENCE OF TREES

One early Saturday morning, Tyler called one of my friends and me, asking if we wanted to go out of town for lunch and hang out with him and his friend Andrew from the Midnight Martyrs. I relished the opportunity and was eager to spend time with a good friend and some strong mentors who were stirring my heart for the things of God. We knew that wherever Tyler went, there was a good chance he'd end up sharing the gospel or having an impromptu sermon on a street corner. Tyler told us to make sure that we had our Bibles along with us at all times, ready to go. It didn't feel like the guys were really pushing to mentor us; they had a true gift of discipleship and somehow found a way to genuinely make us feel like we were friends and a part of their group, all while pouring into us.

Tyler and Andrew picked us up in their car, and we drove north for about 20 minutes or so past the city limits when Tyler said, "Let's just drive and see where we end up."

I started thinking that maybe Tyler and Andrew didn't have an agenda after all. Since I just wanted to hang out anyway, I was fine with that. Tyler drove while Andrew read stories from *Foxe's Book of Martyrs,* as it was always inspiring and faith-building. Andrew handed the book back to me and told us to each take a turn reading aloud, so we did.

Shortly after, Tyler noticed a small dirt driveway ahead on the highway going into what looked like a little forest or circle of trees. He said excitedly, "Hey guys, this looks interesting; let's check it out."

Since we wanted to fit in and were feeling a little more adventurous than we would have been on our own, we went along with it. Tyler drove onto the shoulder of the highway and turned right onto the dirt driveway. Hoping we would not get in trouble if this was private property, Tyler parked his vehicle behind some bushes.

My friend and I were unsure about what Tyler was up to, and I was actually a little nervous that a police officer would come by and we would be in trouble for trespassing. I remember saying, "You think this is okay? It might be private."

My question was cut off by the sound of the car doors opening. "Come on, and bring your Bibles!" Tyler ordered.

We stepped out of the car and walked several metres down the deserted dirt driveway. As we made our way past a few bushes and shrubs, we came upon the circle of tall poplar trees that we observed when driving in. In the middle of this circle of trees was a small pond.

We asked Tyler what we were doing in this place and he replied, "Scripture says that we are to go to all the world and preach the gospel, and I'm pretty sure no one has ever preached the gospel in this spot. We could be the first ones! Besides, declaring the word of God to the atmosphere—to nature and the trees— actually changes the atmosphere and blesses the Lord's heart, and it's a great way to learn to preach. So, let's preach! Find a Scripture that you want to speak from and be ready to go when I'm done."

Tyler made his way to the other side of the pond where he could take his "pulpit," and Andrew stood to the left of us. My friend and I just quietly stood together, trying to look like we were cool with this whole scenario. Tyler then began to preach, reading from Psalm 19: *The heavens declare the glory of God, the skies proclaim the work of his hands.*

While he was speaking, my friend and I were frantically searching for a Scripture from which to preach our spontaneous sermons. Andrew took the pulpit next and started pacing as if there were a thousand people watching as he preached. He started with a story about a Puritan preacher and the start of a major revival. When his time was up after an inspiring seven minute sermon, it was my turn.

I don't remember which passage of Scripture I ended up using, but I'm pretty sure that my sermon lasted all of forty-five seconds. It was neither inspiring nor stirring, but it was still the Word of God spoken out loud to the atmosphere.

This whole story seems so bizarre to people who have heard it, but there was something about standing around that pond together that felt significant. We may not have preached to the masses and seen salvation in that place, but we declared the Word of the Lord back to Him and, in the process of practising our preaching, planted seeds of truth and authority in our own hearts.

The point is not that my sermon lasted forty-five seconds, but that I discovered I didn't need a crowd of people in front of me to be a preacher, evangelist or even a worship leader. I could simply do it. I could find an audience of trees or waves on a lake and simply declare the truths of God, the glory of God and the attributes of God before His beautiful creation. Not only would it hone my skills in preaching and change the atmosphere, but it would become real and alive in my own heart as well, and I would be blessing the heart of the Lord.

After that day I made several additional excursions on my own, finding a deserted spot or taking a quick hike into the forest while on camping trips to preach and sing. I remember at that time in my life getting so much more out of the Word of God, so much more revelation, and so much more authority to share the gospel with my friends.

CAMP

That same year I went to a summer camp. I took my Bible with me everywhere, and I didn't want to do anything at camp that wasn't centred on God. While everyone else played basketball, football or soccer, I would leave the main camp area and preach to the trees. My friends and fellow campers were curious about why I disappeared during these times. One day a few of them quietly followed me into the trees to see what I was up to. I found a beautiful little spot among some pine trees and started my sermon. I didn't even know I was preaching to anybody until I finished and turned around to walk back. They stared at me in bewilderment. One of the girls in the group (who I don't believe was walking with the Lord) got straight to the point, asking, "Why are you yelling at those trees?"

My hunger for the Lord was contagious, and the campers who followed me into the woods that day bombarded me with Bible questions and started following me around the camp. I began to understand how Jesus felt when He tried to be alone with God, only to have people follow Him everywhere. I did not seek to minister to people, but they ended up seeking out a minister. The truths of the Word spoken back to God changed the atmosphere in the camp and brought hearts closer to Him. All I had to do was minister to the Lord. He would do the rest.

A MAN AFTER GOD'S OWN HEART

Preaching to the trees gave me a better understanding of what it was like for David. God was seeking a man after His own heart. This sounds like few would qualify. One would assume that it must be someone with influence, power and authority, or a major prophet with a huge ministry. But when God sought out a man after His own heart, He found a shepherd boy in a field. David spent the first part of his life gazing over fields singing, ministering and meditating over an audience of sheep. My sheep just happened to be trees instead—and, I might add, a lot easier to manage!

When Samuel went to the home of Jesse and invited Jesse and his sons (seven of them) to the sacrifice and the anointing, David was not invited. Instead, he stayed with the sheep. David wasn't even part of the conversation until Samuel looked at all the brothers without finding the right man and had to ask, "Are there any others?"

Jesse then responded, "There remains yet the youngest, and there he is, keeping the sheep."(1 Samuel 16:11)

David sought favour with God, not with man. The fact that Jesse was able to point at David and say, ". . . and there he is," tells us that David wasn't far off and was likely to see the activity happening with his father and brothers. David did not run to the house when he saw the great prophet coming. He did not put on a big orange shirt and say, "Look at me!" David did not come seeking to be part of the process. David chose to stay with the sheep. He sought God apart from everyone else. This resulted in God seeking him out, prompting Samuel to ask, "Are *all* the young men here?" The long days David spent singing to the Lord while tending to the sheep was the training ground that God used to raise up a worshipper for Himself and a king for His people. When God anoints someone, they don't need to seek out ministry to find it; God finds them!

Not only did God seek out a man after his own heart and find David, but also King Saul sought after a man who was skilled in playing the harp to relieve him of a distressing spirit, and he found David, too. Here's what amazes me the most: where did the king's servants find David when Saul sent for him? The servants found him with the sheep! (1 Samuel 16:19)

Even after David was anointed the future king by Samuel, he did not go off to some internship or school to learn how to become king; he stayed at his father's house. He remained a diligent servant, vigilantly watching over the sheep day after day, hour after hour, tending to them and singing to God. What was it that kept him there? What kept him steady in the mundane? David knew that God's presence was always with him (Psalm 139).

David was the best example apart from Christ Himself of what it means to live before the Audience of One. He never parted from the anchor of His life which was his desire to be before God alone, giving Him all the glory, and gazing upon the beauty of the Lord.

DAVID'S TABERNACLE:
FACILITATING THE AUDIENCE OF ONE PARADIGM

'After this I will return and will rebuild the tabernacle of David, which has fallen down;

I will rebuild its ruins, and I will set it up;

So that the rest of mankind may seek the Lord, even all the Gentiles who are called by My name, says the Lord, who does all these things.'

-Acts 15:16-17

God did not say He was going to establish the tabernacle of Moses or the tabernacle of Solomon; God desires and will rebuild the tabernacle of David. Why did God choose it this way? *". . . that the rest of mankind may seek the Lord . . ."(Acts 15:17)*. Why was David's tabernacle an ideal place to seek the Lord? David put a lot of the ceremonial items to the side, even ignoring the structure of the temple itself, to focus on the Lord's presence. David made the ark of the presence of the Lord the focus. Around it he placed hundreds of singers and thousands of musicians to minister at their appointed times to the presence of the Lord day and night. God's heart was moved by the endless supply of worship rising up before Him, and He wanted it to be a model for when He returns.

Even the latter Kings of Israel—Jehoshaphat, Hezekiah, and Josiah—caught on and attempted to follow the Davidic model.

God will one day rebuild a physical temple on the earth, and we will see churches modeled after the tabernacle of David all around the earth. But for now, our bodies are the temple of God, and the Spirit of God that lives within us is transforming our hearts to make Him the centre of it all. He is restoring worship in spirit and in truth. He wants there to be an endless supply of incense from our hearts rising up to Him alone.

David received a revelation in his heart of the worship in heaven—the Revelation 4 type of worship. I am convinced that David had a heavenly experience that caused him to earnestly long for the establishment of God's house on earth. It likely fuelled his tenacity.

> *I will not give sleep to my eyes*
> *or slumber to my eyelids, until I find a place for the Lord,*
> *A dwelling place for the Mighty One of Jacob.*

-Psalm 132:4-5

CARRYING OUR HEARTS LIKE DAVID

When it comes to the heart, everybody sits on a level playing field, and the Lord looks at how we carry it and our intentions. If we seek after big ministry and a name for ourselves, we will receive man's honour, but there are greater rewards for those who seek the Lord's heart in the secret place and whose primary desire and intention is to bring Him all the glory, honour and praise, rather than praise and glory to themselves.

There is a difference between getting glory and receiving encouragement. I struggled with this distinction for many years. I didn't want the spotlight; I wanted my actions to put *God* in the spotlight. This was true even when I did not fully comprehend the Audience of One paradigm. It got to the point where I did not know how to respond when people tried to encourage me.

I had to bring this to the Lord because I know there is nothing wrong with receiving encouragement; in fact, this is one of the purposes for Christians to meet together. When I brought it to the Lord, I realized that every encouragement I received was an opportunity to bring glory to God and to thank Him for making me a vessel to be used for His purposes. Encouragement helps us to flourish in the assignments that He gives us. It is fuel for the fire.

Personal glory, however, goes beyond encouragement and puts us in the spotlight. Giving glory to someone is telling them that they have something to offer apart from God. We can give glory to God because He has everything to offer apart from anyone or anything. But we can't give encouragement to God. Why would God need encouragement? He is self motivated and self sustaining. Do we see the difference? Encouragement is for man, glory is for God.

It is wrong to give to and receive glory from another person. You can't control what people think of you, only how you carry your heart before the Lord. There were people worshipping, singing songs and dancing in the streets in the name of David and, not only that, they were singing their songs in front of the authorities and powers of the day (King Saul), parading David's name and shouting out accolades.

Now it had happened as they were coming home,
when David was returning from the slaughter of the
Philistine, that the women had come out of all the cities
of Israel, singing and dancing, to meet King Saul, with
tambourines, with joy, and with musical instruments. So
the women sang as they danced, and said:

"Saul has slain his thousands,
And David his ten thousands."

-1 Samuel 18:6-7 (NIV)

David remained humble in the midst of it; he neither asked for glory nor did he condone it. In 1 Samuel 18, it says that David did as he was told and behaved wisely. In other words, David carried his heart well in the midst of victory and favour. David was esteemed by men because of the way he positioned his heart, but his primary desire was to be esteemed by God.

So David went out wherever Saul sent him, and behaved wisely. And Saul set him over the men of war, and he was accepted in the sight of all the people and also in the sight of Saul's servants.

-1 Samuel 18:5

Then the princes of the Philistines went out to war. And so it was, whenever they went out, that David behaved more wisely than all the servants of Saul, so that his name became highly esteemed.

-1 Samuel 18:30

This was not something David just stumbled into; he lived this way intently:

I will behave wisely in a perfect way.
Oh, when will You come to me?
I will walk within my house with a perfect heart.

I will set nothing wicked before my eyes
I hate the work of those who fall away;
It shall not cling to me.

A perverse heart shall depart from me;
I will not know wickedness.

-Psalm 101:2-4

What a wonderful picture the Scripture gives us through the life of David on how to carry our hearts humbly and to have the Lord be a praise on the earth! David continually put himself before the Audience of One, and living to bring God glory remained burning on his heart throughout his life and ministry.

David's devotional life is a blueprint for the type of people God seeks. God wants to raise up shepherds looking over the fields on the Lord's beauty, a royal priesthood and a holy nation.

And I will give you shepherds according to My heart, who will feed you with knowledge and understanding.

-Jeremiah 3:15

God is looking for a kingdom of people who are after His heart. He's searching the earth for people who, like David, are priestly in ministry and will give God all the glory in the midst of praises, trouble and promises. He desires to have people who will not be swayed by sin but will run into His arms wholeheartedly. Scripture tells us that He provided David as a witness to us (Isaiah 55:4).

God desires us to set our eyes on heaven and eternal things. He seeks people who have a longing to see the worship that is taking place in heaven be established on the earth. They are people who have caught a glimpse of Him, and nothing else will do but to behold the beauty of the Lord, to stand before Him and minister to His heart alone. This is the invitation to each and every believer.

One thing I have desired of the Lord,
That will I seek:
That I may dwell in the house of the Lord
All the days of my life,

To behold the beauty of the Lord,
And to inquire in His temple.

-Psalm 27:4

David's primary goal and main desire was to stand in the Lord's presence. These are the words of a king and prophet, not someone who has nothing to lose. David was seeking out the life of a priest while living the life of a king.

What does gazing upon the beauty of the Lord have to do with the Audience of One paradigm? In the throne room there are angels, elders and living creatures all gazing upon the One on the throne. God desires all creation to gaze with fascination upon His beauty. This brings glory to Himself. When God becomes the object of our affections, He becomes all that we are living and breathing for. He becomes our obsession, passion and desire.

When we behold Him, we become ruined for anything else.

Make it the cry of my heart not to give rest to my eyes until
there is a resting place for You, Lord . . . a place where You are
worshipped and have incense arising to you day and night.
This one thing I desire: to gaze upon Your beauty
all the days of my life.

The most valuable thing the Psalms do for me is to express the same delight in God which made David dance.

-C.S. Lewis

FIVE

PRIESTLY MONIKERS & SECRET IDENTITIES

Whenever the words *priesthood, David* or *tabernacle* come up in conversation, heads turn in my direction. The people who know me have heard some of the prophetic words spoken over me, which often involve the subjects stated above, and they also know that I am passionate about these things. I know that I *am* a priest before the Lord, and He has spoken David's story and revealed his heart to me in a way that has become part of my lifestyle. I am going to attempt to lay out what the priesthood means to me and how it has affected my life.

First, I'm going to address the following question: What are priests, and what do they have to do with the Audience of One paradigm?

Simply:

1. God is the audience.

2. Worship is the activity.

3. Priests are the ones who perform this activity.

To live an Audience of One lifestyle means to be a priest. Now, before you dismiss this, remember that Jesus himself is called a priest.

> *Seeing then that we have a great High Priest who has passed through the heavens, Jesus the Son of God, let us hold fast our confession.*

-Hebrews 4:14

Throughout most of my life, the concept of being a priest was foreign to me. When I first heard the word *priest*, I automatically pictured a Catholic priest with a white collar offering forgiveness of sin in a confessional booth. It felt disconnected from my context, and I didn't think it was relevant to me. I knew that priests could not marry (and I wanted a family), and this did not appeal to me at all. I knew there were priests in the Scriptures, especially the Old Testament.

I never gave a second thought to the significance of God's priestly calling for me and for His church in general. It never crossed my mind that I would have a priestly calling on my life and, in fact, that it would become my identity and how I would define my heart and ministry.

Though there are many similarities between priests and monks, I found myself drawn more to the fasted lifestyle of monks before I received a revelation of what a priest actually was.

Whenever I watched the movie *Robin Hood*, I found myself cheering on Friar Tuck rather than Robin. Monks fascinated me, but I wasn't really interested in becoming one. It was more of a fantasy and a romanticism of their lifestyle that garnered my interest—lives spent studying and copying old manuscripts, and living in simplicity and devotion to God. I still receive words about not only the priestly call on my life, but that I am a monk as well.

THE CHANT OF MONKS

One day at school in one of our Bible classes, we were learning about the history and development of the Church. Our Bible teacher brought in some audio tapes of Gregorian chants. Our class mumbled and quietly groaned when we heard the teacher describing what she was about to play for us. We all wanted to be Christian rock stars, and some old monks chanting songs that we could not understand was not exactly something that appealed to teenage boys.

But we didn't really have a say, so our teacher put the tape in. It began with a quiet, male voice singing a low, droning melody in what sounded like Latin. A choir of males joined in the song, echoing the opening melody. Then came a series of responsive echoes, singing something different each time. It was so dynamic and brooding, yet there were no instruments. It was just voices.

I was completely captivated by what I heard that day. The sound of the monk's voices, their echoes and responses, stirred something in my heart. Though I could not understand a word, somehow my spirit understood; it went beyond language. The melodies and harmonies blended together for one purpose: to bring glory to God. The sounds brought my very soul to the heights of heaven, placing me before the throne on the sea of glass, worshipping with the saints and angels there. It is what I would describe as the ancient glory of God.

I began to get lost in what I was hearing and put my head down on my desk. As I closed my eyes, a scene began to unfold in my mind. I saw a picture of a monastery carved out of the top of a mountain cliff. Inside there was a large, empty hall of stone where a group of monks in simple brown tunics were all singing songs from piles of scrolls containing the Psalms of David. They would choose one of the scrolls and sing the Psalm together and, even though they sang these songs every day, I could see the life on them. There seemed to be revelation the monks discovered through repetition, and there was joy in it all.

Then I saw myself singing among them. There was no one in the room to hear us. We were all just singing as part of our duty, yet it was our delight. The whole scene was elaborate and romantic, yet simple and joyful. At the time, I did not fully understand why this picture came to me and why it was so impacting.

Looking back, I now understand that it was another seed the Lord planted in me to develop my identity to be before Him alone in worship. He was drawing my heart into an Audience of One lifestyle of praying, searching out the Word, fasting and singing. In this one vision, the Lord defined for me what He wanted from my heart and life.

While this experience stayed in the back of my mind over the years, I knew I couldn't time travel back several centuries and become a monk. I didn't even know if they still existed in any part of the world. Either way, it would be strange going from being a Pentecostal pastor's kid to a monk on a mountain.

Years later, I went to look at some CD's in a music store. I don't know what prompted me to go to the world music section, but while I was browsing, a compact disc with a picture of a monastery atop a lush green cliff caught my eye. It was entitled *The World of Gregorian Chant*. Loud enough to catch the attention of those around me in the store (louder than I intended) I exclaimed, "No way!"and immediately snagged the lone copy off the shelf.

The mental picture I got that day in the classroom suddenly flooded back into my mind, and there it was in my hands. I felt the same stirring in my heart when I picked up the CD as I did back in that high school classroom. I bought it immediately, and I remember lying on my bed with my eyes closed and listening while the chants played. I would replay the vision in my head over and over. It was a precious gift from the Lord and a reminder that there was something about the lifestyle of the monks that was for me.

PRIEST DAVID

For as long as I can remember, David has been an important biblical figure in my life. Since the age of three, I wanted to be a singer and worship leader, and David's life significantly influenced those goals.

What I didn't fully grasp until later in life was that David wasn't just a worship leader turned king. David was a priest and actually organized a whole generation of priests to minister before the

Lord. His primary purpose in life was to be before God, and he wanted his generation to experience the same reality and revelation of purpose.

Although I wasn't specifically trying to imitate David's lifestyle, I started seeing many similarities and comparisons. I realized that I was drawn to the priestly aspects of David's life story. It was through studying David's lifestyle that I finally saw what the Lord desired from true priestly ministry. My clouded, modern perception of the priesthood became much clearer.

When I joined the house of prayer, I frequently heard the language of the priesthood, and it defined for me what it truly meant to be a priest. It started making sense to me and, at the same time, it began marking my heart.

While the term *priest* is common in my church circle, it's easy to forget that the language of the priesthood is still largely lost on the majority of Protestants. We still get funny looks sometimes when we mention being a priest to other church leaders or members outside our church family. It's easy to lose people altogether because they don't initially understand what we mean.

The Protestant church has found new terms to describe the priesthood by calling someone a pastor, elder or worship leader. I am convinced that the Lord will reclaim the term *priest* for His purposes in all expressions of His church. He wants to and will remove all the false perceptions and any negative connotations attached to what a priest is and does.

Until we understand the value in God's heart for His priests, we will undervalue and remain disconnected with His plans and purposes for every Christian. No one who loves Jesus is only a pastor, worship leader, elder, doctor, teacher or counsellor, etc.

Whatever our earthly occupation and whatever title we hold, it is our highest call and our greatest joy to be priests before God, ministering to His heart above all.

PRIESTLY REWARDS

The priestly lifestyle goes against the grain of life. It can be offensive to the human heart and mind. Humans don't naturally direct all glory and attention away from themselves. Priests choose to live in simplicity and in the secret place with God as their Audience of One so that God receives all the glory from their lives.

A priestly lifestyle does not entitle us to power, great wealth or influence among men—not in this age anyway. The only thing priests are entitled to is the Lord Himself, just as He promised the Levitical priests.

"It shall be, in regard to their inheritance, that I am their inheritance. You shall give them no possession in Israel, for I am their possession."

-Ezekiel 44:28

It is the greatest reward we as priests could ask for. It's our blessed hope and fulfilment of our destiny in Christ. And as we see in this verse, the Lord has taken what was held back from the priests and saved it as an eternal reward. So not only will we have the Lord as our possession, but we will receive land to rule alongside Him as well.

"For You were slain,
And have redeemed us to God by Your blood

Out of every tribe and tongue and people and nation, And have made us kings and priests to our God; And we shall reign on the earth. "

-Revelation 5:9b-10

THE ARK OF THE COVENANT

My favourite movie of all time is *Raiders of the Lost Ark*. Because of that movie, I grew to love history and, more specifically, biblical history and the Ark of the Covenant. The ark became my hobby, and I bought books and documentaries about it. Even as I write this, there is a model Ark of the Covenant on my desk in front of me.

I wanted to know what happened to the ark. Where might it be today? Did it have eternal implications? Will we see it again? What was it about this box that was so important to God? Would it still have the same power today as it did back then?

While I have many theories related to these questions, the point is that the ark bore the presence of the Lord. The priests ministered before the ark. From that gold box they saw a cloud of glory appear, and it filled the temple. They knew this was where the Lord was dwelling in their midst, and they recognized the necessity to have a priest minister before the presence of God.

Why was it only the Levites who could carry the ark, bearing the literal presence of the Lord on their shoulders? The priests understood the need to be consecrated and holy in order to minister before the Lord. Sacrifices had to be made; hands needed to be cleansed.

While there is no ark today for us to minister before, one thing hasn't changed: the necessity for God to be ministered to by priests. It is important to Him to have priestly people minister to Him, so much so that He made Himself far more accessible to us than He ever was to those in the Old Testament.

First, He calls us all priests so that we can all bear His presence. It is living inside us through the Holy Spirit, never far away! Second, He sent Jesus to die so that we could enter into the Most Holy Place. If He sent His own Son to die, what does it say about how He feels about us accessing His presence?

ALL ARE CALLED TO BE PRIESTS

We are all called to be priests before the Lord. It's on the Lord's heart to raise up a kingdom of priests so that every believer brings pleasure to God in whatever they do. He desires people who are set apart to walk in holiness before Him, lovers who will agree with His heart and declare God's praise in the earth. He is the King and His subjects are to be priests.

> *But you are a chosen people, a royal priesthood, a holy nation, God's special possession, that you may declare the praises of him who called you out of darkness into his wonderful light;*
>
> -1 Peter 2:9

> *". . . and from Jesus Christ, the faithful witness, the firstborn from the dead, and the ruler over the kings of the earth.*
> *To Him who loved us and washed us from our sins in His own blood, and has made us kings and priests to His God*

*and Father, to Him be glory and dominion forever and
ever. Amen."*

-Revelation 1:5-6

The Lord put His stamp on His people, both Jews and Gentiles, and called them priests. This calling commissions us to seek Him in all that we do as our first objective in bringing Him glory. If we desire to stand in His temple and gaze upon the King, we must have the title of a priest.

Only His priests were permitted to go into the Holy of Holies. He has qualified us all to enter into His presence by calling us priests through Jesus' shed blood.

There are some who are called to be priests as their vocation, ones who keep the spiritual fire on the altar burning day and night in a specific physical location set apart for this purpose. The Lord is worthy and *should* have people glorifying Him unceasingly. We need these ones to facilitate a spiritual burning altar where all others could come to meet with the Lord. We need to create houses of prayer for them to live out their priestly call.

Not everybody has the ability or call to do so as their vocation, but all are called to do their jobs within the priestly identity. God desires to have priestly doctors, teachers, salespeople, law enforcement workers, government employees, moms and dads, pastors, missionaries and evangelists . . . the list goes on. Not one job is more important than another, but all have their place in the kingdom of priests, and all are meant to bring God glory. Whatever we do, it is intended for one purpose: to bring glory, honour and praise unto the Lord.

*Bondservants, obey in all things your masters according
to the flesh, not with eye service, as men-pleasers, but*

in sincerity of heart, fearing God. And whatever you do,
do it heartily, as to the Lord and not to men, knowing
that from the Lord you will receive the reward of the
inheritance; for you serve the Lord Christ.

-Colossians 3:22-24

David wrote most of the Psalms and established a worship and prayer movement that would have long-range influence on the temples built thereafter. David even took government money and resources to ensure there was worship in the temple day and night. It was an essential service.

As king, David had many jobs to occupy his time, including decisions on warfare, taxation, land divisions and disputes. With all the responsibility, authority and power that David possessed, what is the one thing he desired? He longed to be a priest and to spend his days looking at God. Look at this verse again:

One thing I have desired of the Lord,
That will I seek:
That I may dwell in the house of the Lord
All the days of my life,
To behold the beauty of the Lord,
And to inquire in His temple.

-Psalm 27:4

David understood that God was the one who placed him in his position of authority specifically because of his priestly heart. God created a king out of a man who was found in the place of gazing upon the One in full authority over the universe.

Where do you think a shepherd boy got boldness and authority to rule over a nation and defeat armies? He spent his life watching the Most High God do it. He lived his life not before men, but before God. He had a wonderful gift of meekness that kept God at the centre of all the increase in authority, wealth and favour.

OUR JOBS AS PRIESTS

God requires pure priests committed to obeying the commands of his heart. Priests are to be holy in order to enter the Holy of Holies. God requires a pure bride offering unblemished worship. It is downright impossible to attain to this high standard without the grace of God. We are called to be a holy people belonging to God. We are not just guests invited in, but we are His bride and we belong to Him. He wants us in close proximity to Him.

Those who are near to Him must be holy, just as He is holy. If we are asked to declare His holiness, we ourselves must be holy. He is a jealous husband who desires our full love and attention. As our husband, He longs to dwell with His bride, and this desire should stir up our desire to be holy and one with Him.

Just as God calls us a royal priesthood, God also calls us a holy nation. In other words, people set apart who are under the authority of the King, belonging to Him alone. Around His throne, the four living creatures never stop saying, "Holy, holy, holy." He wants the same thing from His priests on earth as it is in heaven. He is establishing dwelling places around the earth where people can minister to Him as priests, as holy people who will declare Him to be the Holy One.

> *". . . This is what the Lord spoke, saying:*
> *'By those who come near Me*
> *I must be regarded as holy;*

And before all the people
I must be glorified."'

-Leviticus 10:3

Priests need fire on the altar to have constant praise arising to God. Just as the priests offered up incense and mixed spices to make a new aroma and offering to the Lord, we present a mixture of devotion, songs, prayers, voluntary love, desire and fascination as our offering to the Lord. The difference between the Old Testament priesthood and the priesthood the Lord is establishing today is that now God dwells inside human beings and not temples made by human hands.

In the Old Testament, there were a lot of things the priests had to carry out according to their duties. Now we have to carry certain things pertaining to the heart. This is why Jesus spoke so often about the issues of the heart. He dwells within our hearts through the Holy Spirit. He even said it would be better for Him to leave so that the helper, the Holy Spirit, would come. He knew that He could be even closer than He was when He came in the flesh. If only we realized the longing in God's heart to be close to us! Our priorities would be profoundly different.

THE OFFICE OF THE PRIEST

"And when you pray, you shall not be like the hypocrites.
For they love to pray standing in the synagogues and on
the corners of the streets, that they may be seen by men.
Assuredly, I say to you, they have their reward."

-Matthew 6:5

The secret place is the office of the priest. This is where business gets done, where the priest desires to spend the majority of his time and energy. This is not a physical structure, but rather a heart posture, where all our energy is spent on the sole purpose of bringing glory to Jesus by beholding His beauty.

I've heard stories about monks of old living in complete seclusion within the confines of a room not much larger than the size of their cot. The room had no door and was enclosed by bricks with a small opening in the wall to receive their daily rations of food and water. They spent all of their time meditating on Scripture, praying, talking to God and giving Him all their love, devotion and attention. When they died, the room became their tomb. The small opening was closed in with brick and mortar.

I am not suggesting we start locking each other in doorless rooms, but there is a heart posture evident here that is dear to the Lord. There is something to be said for a life wasted on Jesus.

David said that zeal for God's house consumed him (Psalm 69), and he would not rest until he found a dwelling place for the Lord. What a wonderful invitation there is for us to use our time and energy to minister to God where He is our one and only divine audience, our Audience of One! The reward is immeasurable.

Thank You, God, for making me a priest, that I might enter
into Your Presence with boldness. Let me besatisfied withthe
goodness of Your house.
You are my great reward and my inheritance.

God's purpose for my life was that I have
a passion for God's glory and that I have
a passion for my joy in that glory, and that
these two are one passion.

-Jonathan Edwards

SIX

TREASURES & PLEASURES

Through the ages the question at the centre of humanity has been, what is my purpose? Or, why am I here? The answer has been staring mankind in the face. It has always been there in the Holy Scriptures, waiting for us to read plainly and believe. The problem we have is that the answer is theocentric (God-centred) rather than egocentric (self-centred). It is contrary to our natural inclination to look out for number one. However, our very existence and value are intricately linked to the relationship we have with our Creator.

"You are worthy, O Lord,
To receive glory and honour and power;

For You created all things,
And by Your will they exist and were created."

-Revelation 4:11

The greatest treasure we can receive is found in fulfilling our life's purpose. That purpose is fulfilled in bringing glory and pleasure to Jesus.

Therefore we make it our aim, whether present or absent,
to be well pleasing to Him.

-2 Corinthians 5:9

God could have created creatures that fulfilled this purpose perfectly. He easily could have created creatures that neither sinned in the garden nor rebelled. He could have created robots that would never once lose focus on their main objective, that would not waiver or grow weary.

So why did He not do it that way? Why did He create humans whom He already knew were going to fall? Why did God, in all His perfection, create man in His image, only for man to defile His image? The reason He created us this way is that He wanted glory for Himself offered not out of obligation, but out of voluntary love and affection. God wanted love from weak and broken vessels. It was and is His pleasure to receive worship and voluntary love from weak creatures that will continually strive and struggle to give it to Him. Not only is it His pleasure, but it is also for His glory to do so.

Let's think about this for a moment. There is actually something God cannot have unless we give it to Him, and it is the one thing He wants from us. When we give Him our voluntary love, He rewards us with treasures and pleasures unending that we cannot even begin to repay.

"Who has ever given to God, that God should repay them?"

-Romans 11:35 (NIV)

If we look at 1 Corinthians 2:9, it should blow our minds because there is a huge treasure trove of rewards that we don't yet know about. There are mysteries in the treasures prepared for us in heaven.

"Eye has not seen, nor ear heard,
Nor have entered into the heart of man
The things which God has prepared for those
who love Him."

-1 Corinthians 2:9

The fact is, God doesn't need us, but He deeply desires to have us as His own. There is nothing greater, nothing higher that any created being can receive than the love, affections, attention and desires of their creator and God. We are the object of His affection. We hold a place in His heart higher than any other created thing. He included us in the experiential love between Jesus and the Father. The same love that the Father has for the Son, He has for us (John 15:9).

It is His desire that it would be like it was in the garden at the dawn of creation. This was His intention in creating us, that we would be by His side. How is it possible for the King with all His power and authority to have lowly servants by His side? He doesn't call us servants, but He calls us friends and makes us kings and priests to rule and reign with Him.

If that's not enough to convince us of His desire to be close to us, He goes a step further and calls us His bride and is even now preparing a wedding. What greater reward is there than a wedding celebration with our creator and being by His side, ruling and reigning with Him?

THE PLEASURES OF FASCINATION

What about the treasure of awe? We humans love to be amazed. God has created us to be fascinated and astonished. He loves to be seen, and it brings Him glory when He fascinates those around Him. Fascination comes by looking at Him and digging into the depths of his beauty and character. The deeper we delve into the heart of God to discover and be fascinated by His beauty, the more treasure we will find. The beauty of Jesus is like a towering mountain filled with precious gems, and we get to spend eternity mining its inexhaustible treasures.

There is reward in searching and uncovering the mysteries of God. When walking out the Audience of One lifestyle, we find joy in the searching and finding, the digging and uncovering, and the gazing and adoring.

The deeper we look into those eyes of fire, the more we realize that we have not even begun to understand or grasp the depths of God. The more we seek to know His heart, His thoughts and His emotions, the more we realize that we have just scratched the surface. In time we will find that even though we are getting more revelation, the scratch has not gone any deeper. The mystery and perpetual search and discovery drives us to desperation to know the man, Jesus. It creates people who want to be before Him, never to depart from that place of gazing at Him.

> *. . . that their hearts may be encouraged, being knit together in love, and attaining to all riches of the full assurance of understanding, to the knowledge of the*

mystery of God, both of the Father and of Christ, in whom are hidden all the treasures of wisdom and knowledge.

-Colossians 2:2-3

Nothing compares to the privilege and pleasure found in gazing on the transcendent beauty of the living God. One of the roles of a priest is quite simply to look at God. God loves to be looked at because He has so much beauty that must be seen.

He put living creatures around His throne with eyes all around them to perform the primary function of taking in what they see. They have been in that place longer than we can begin to fathom, and they are not yet bored or tired; neither have they exhausted the wells of fascination that are found in God. They never refrain from saying, "Holy, holy, holy, Lord God Almighty, who was and is and is to come!"

Why do these creatures never get bored of saying it over and over? Is not doing the same thing over and over the very essence of boredom? The key is, when you are looking upon the uncreated God of the universe, it is impossible to be bored. The four living creatures keep falling down over and over because they see something of God that drives them to endless fascination. He is so holy and so higher than, that their natural response is to fall down and get low.

If the four living creatures had a mom calling them to come eat supper, they would be perpetually saying, "Just five more minutes . . . the show isn't over." I have never once watched a movie or experienced an event that caused me to fall on my face in fascination and awe.

Our eyes have become so dull that we try to take the easy route and fascinate ourselves with the things around us. There is an invitation for us to be awed by looking at Jesus; however, it requires so much more of us. But the reward is immeasurable!

Lest we think God is uninteresting, we need to realize what utterly dull creatures we are. We get restless in a one or two-hour worship set. If there are creatures in heaven with eyes all around them that are always fascinated by God, why is it that we get so quickly distracted with our two eyes?

Our lack of revelation should rattle us to the core and cause us to cry out for more. It's not that God is stingy in revealing more of Himself; He is generous and will give us as much as we want. We just don't want enough. Just as God gave the four living creatures eyes all around to behold Him, if we posture ourselves before Him, He will open our eyes to reveal more.

TREASURES IN BEAUTY

People love beautiful things. We were made to admire beauty; we love art, music, decoration and fashion. God has surrounded Himself with all of these things, but they are more beautiful than any of us can imagine. The beauty surrounding Him is all focused on revealing things about Himself. It is transcendent beauty and is intended to be perpetually fascinating to us. It is our pleasure and our greatest treasure to behold this beauty and to spend eternity plunging the depths of its endless wells.

So what exactly is it that makes Him so beautiful? What makes Him so fascinating? Only the Holy Spirit reveals God, and it's our privilege, our pleasure and, more so, our *glory* to seek Him out and find out who He is. No other creatures on this earth have this privilege.

VISION OF A CROWN

Eternal rewards await us in heaven based on how we live our lives on earth. When I was five years old, I was fortunate to see one of my rewards in advance. It happened in the north-central Saskatchewan community of Prince Albert in 1987, but I remember it like it was yesterday. After a typical day of playing with little green plastic army men, imagining myself becoming the next professional football player, and pretending to be a mean giant who ravages a village of ants by squishing them underfoot, I fell soundly asleep in my bedroom wrapped under a warm blanket. Everyone had retired for the night, and the house and air were still. Little did I know that within the next few minutes, I would be awakened by a visitor in my room, and I would see something that would stick with me forever.

Who's touching my shoulder? I stirred slightly and continued sleeping. It happened again, and I wondered whose gentle hand was trying to wake me up. Mom? Dad? It was still dark, and I was tired and not yet ready to wake up.

My confused body finally shook free from its deep slumber. I opened my eyes, but no one was there. I quickly became fixated on what was beyond the foot of my bed. My heart skipped a beat in my chest, and I rubbed my eyes and reminded myself to breathe.

There on my wall was an illuminated image. Just like a projector displaying a motion picture on my wall, I saw the most dazzling and exquisite crown one could lay eyes on. It was shining gold and bright, spinning around and around, with glistening rubies, emeralds, sapphires and other precious stones. The most affluent king would be exceedingly fortunate to have such a crown.

Terrified and confused, I sat and stared at this mysterious picture. As beautiful and captivating as it was, it was not something a small child would consider a normal thing to wake up to. I looked behind me for a projector, but there was nothing, and I came to the realization that I was not dreaming.

What could I do? My door was a few feet away from the spinning crown. My fear of staying in my room outweighed my dread of getting any closer to the image for a quick escape. I crawled out of my bed and pressed my body flat against the wall in order to keep as much distance between me and the crown as possible. I shimmied my way down the wall, dodging furniture and dirty laundry on the floor, and made my way toward the door, not for a moment taking my eyes off of the crown to make sure it would not move closer toward me. I finally reached the door and scurried to Mom and Dad's closed door amid much tears and whimpering.

Imagine my parents trying to explain what I just encountered. I don't think they even fully understood what it meant. All I needed to hear from them was that Jesus showed me a picture. When I heard this I felt like I was given a gift before Christmas, that I was shown something quite special. What I saw that night planted a foundation in my heart for the reality of God. I actually saw one of the eternal rewards that He has fashioned especially for me.

If we understand crowns in Scripture, they are given for specific reasons. I believe I only discovered the reason for the crown in my vision in the last couple of years, and it has direct relationship to living an Audience of One lifestyle.

Now there is in store for me the crown of righteousness,
which the Lord, the righteous Judge, will award to me on
that day—and not only to me, but also to all who have
longed for his appearing.

-2 Timothy 4:8 (NIV)

What does this crown have to do with the Audience of One paradigm? The key lies at the end of the verse: *". . . to all who have longed for his appearing."* When God is our audience, and when we spend our life gazing upon His beauty and standing before Him with the sole desire of giving Him glory, we will long for Him to come back and to bring the fullness of who He is in His glory and majesty. We will long for the day of His appearing when the earth is full of His glory.

A crown is one of the rewards of heaven. This is the type of treasure He wants us to go after. Right after the passage in Matthew 6 about praying and fasting in secret, Jesus tells us not to lay up treasures on earth but in heaven. Our activity in this age has a direct effect on what rewards we will receive in heaven. The decisions we make and how we posture ourselves daily is actually an investment in our heavenly rewards.

REWARDS IN SECRET

I love that Jesus gave a promise of rewards for those who seek Him in the secret place. Let's look at what He says in this passage in Matthew:

"And when you pray, you shall not be like the hypocrites.
For they love to pray standing in the synagogues
and on the corners of the streets, that they may be seen by
men. Assuredly, I say to you, they have their reward. But

you, when you pray, go into your room, and when you have shut your door, pray to your Father who is in the secret place; and your Father who sees in secret will reward you openly."

-Matthew 6:5-6

"Moreover, when you fast, do not be like the hypocrites, with a sad countenance. For they disfigure their faces that they may appear to men to be fasting. Assuredly, I say to you, they have their reward."

-Matthew 6:16

These passages are neither a warning nor a rebuke. They are an invitation to receive a greater reward than what men can offer. Jesus was not pointing fingers or sharing His frustration but revealing heart postures about relating to God. He talks about those who would seek out a reward or recognition from men and those who would want to appear as holy and spiritual. If that is what they are after in their prayer life and ministry, then that is what they will get.

However, the invitation is to seek something higher and greater by being rewarded by the Father. He wants to be the one to reward us. He would rather we receive it from Him than from men because He knows how much greater it is for us. He actually cares that we would not miss out on rewards, and that in itself should tell us something about His character.

To this day I long to see the crown again. When I receive it on that glorious day, it will be even more exciting to see the face of the One who will be giving it to me. What expression will He have on His face? What will He say to me? I can only imagine.

THE ART OF BECOMING A WORSHIPPER

There was a long period in my late teens when I thought I would be the next best thing in Christian music. I was privileged to share the stage with whom I considered to be some of the best Christian worship songwriters at that time, and I was surrounded by an amazing artistic community that was sure to rub off on me. I began writing songs at age 11, and it was always something I enjoyed doing. I thought that surely the Lord had put me in this community to become part of such a great culture of emergent Christian music artists.

Some of these artists were in awe of how someone as young as myself could write so many singable worship tunes. I was often encouraged by musicians, friends and others who heard my songs in different settings. People around me always wanted to hear the latest stuff that I was writing.

When I was 16, I was blessed to have a song recorded on a compilation CD that our church released. The CD went on to sell thousands of copies. People who went on mission trips or visits to various countries would return home and tell me they had heard my song in the churches they had visited. Things were looking up for me and the ministry the Lord set before me.

Because I was on a few worship teams, I was invited to the community's artist collective meetings, a place to build community with the artists in our church sphere and to bounce around ideas, share vision, hang out and be artsy. I got to record in the studio with one of the artists, and the meetings gave me further opportunities to hang out with the worship leaders, attend worship retreats and play bass at cafes and church functions.

Sometimes they would bring me along to out-of-province gigs, usually as a bass guitar player, but they all knew that I also liked to write and desired to lead worship. It gave me a lot of exposure to this Christian artistic community, and I was sure that I had found my niche and could flourish in a community such as this.

However, I knew in my heart that it wasn't true. I had a fantasy in my head that things would happen a certain way. Perhaps I could ignore my gut and follow in the footsteps of those cool, artsy people around me. Although I played instruments, wrote songs and went to all the places the worship people went, I clearly remember the day I was at one of these collective meetings and felt so out of place. They were all sitting around talking, and I was by myself wondering if this was as good as it gets for artists in ministry.

I began to question my whole life's pursuits and ambitions. I came to the realization that I was not like them. All of a sudden, I did not feel like an artist and was not even sure if I wanted to do this anymore.

In the fallout of this epiphany, I was distraught and disillusioned. I left the collective meeting very early and went home to my bedroom. In my dejected state, I cried out to God. I remember saying, as if to convince myself to come to terms with its reality, "This doesn't feel right. I don't belong here. I am not an artist. I am NOT an artist." I then began to question the Lord: "Why all these years learning to be a worship leader? Why did I write all these songs? Why did I play in a bunch of bands and pursue this ministry? Why did I spend all this time and sweat building relationship with these artists? Why did they encourage me in the process? Why did *You* give me songs and encourage me in the process?"

After I was done complaining to the Lord, I felt Him graciously say, "You don't even understand who you are." Then something from deep within my soul burst out in revelation. God spoke clearly to my spirit. Within the depths of my heart I heard the Lord firmly say, "I have not called you to be an artist! I have called you to be a worshipper." It was like the roar of a lion within me, shattering lies and defining my heart.

All my questions suddenly vaporized. I began to weep. All the searching and hard work to find my place in the church was now put to rest. The Lord defined my life's call.

All that time was not wasted; it was simply lacking revelation from the Lord's heart. I was spending all my time trying to gain recognition from a group of artists, trying to find a reward in belonging and in riding the coattails of those I knew to gain favour in ministry.

All along, the Lord wanted me to recognize that He was calling me a priest who belonged to Him. He never asked me to pursue the lifestyle of a Christian music artist, but He wanted me for Himself, to simply be before Him. He wanted me to sing, write and minister out of a heart that was pursuing *His* heart and nothing else. The Lord wanted to be my treasure and reward.

He brought to mind King David and questioned me, "Do you think David pursued a life as an artist? Do you think David sought after other songwriters and defined his role by whom he hung out with? Did I seek out an artist or a man after my heart?"

The Lord didn't have to answer those questions for me to know the answers. He often speaks to me that way. Obviously playing music and writing songs makes one an artist. This does not mean that I am not an artist, but the Lord did not want it to be my sole identity. It's life changing when God reveals who we are rather than us trying to define who we are.

There is a trend in a large portion of the church that pushes worship leaders to be rock stars; put on your skinny jeans and pointy Italian leather shoes, turn off the house lights and illuminate the stage. These things are not wrong in themselves, but God doesn't care about any of it. It may make it a more enjoyable experience for people attending, but it doesn't make it more enjoyable for God.

If the goal is to make our worship service look like a concert, if we want to be trendy or have our church produce rock stars, then that will be our reward. If God really is the only audience, lights on the stage are not going to impress Him. We can have all these things in our church, but if they become more important than His presence and blessing His heart, we need to re-evaluate. I can't say what the intentions of people's hearts are, but I do see a trend in the church.

While I enjoy lights and a fun atmosphere, it doesn't define worship. There is so much more to be gained in putting the ark in the middle, making the presence of the Lord our sole focus.

There is no higher treasure than the Lord Himself. He has seated Himself above the heavens and there is nothing higher in created or uncreated order. This is our inheritance and we are His inheritance. It's an inherited relationship, our birthright, if we choose to accept it. We are sons and daughters of the King of the highest order, and there are treasures and storehouses full of rewards to be discovered when we spend our lives gazing upon Him and diligently seeking Him.

But without faith it is impossible to please Him, for he
who comes to God must believe that He is, and that He is
a rewarder of those who diligently seek Him.

-Hebrews 11:6

The Lord wanted to be my treasure. He didn't want my reward
to be community with a bunch of artists, fame or a powerful
ministry. God wanted worship from me and nothing more. I
was looking for joy and satisfaction through serving Him in
public ministry, but little did I know how much joy, satisfaction
and endless treasures I would discover in the secret place. My
heart was fascinated, and it has ruined me for anything less.
Anything less in this case is everything else that is not His beauty.

Your righteousness is like the great mountains;
Your judgements are a great deep;
O Lord, You preserve man and beast.
How precious is Your lovingkindness, O God!
Therefore the children of men put their trust under the
shadow of Your wings.
They are abundantly satisfied with the
fullness of Your house,
And You give them drink from the river of Your pleasures.
For with You is the fountain of life;
In Your light we see light.

-Psalms 36:6-9

Our joy is found at the feet of Jesus, in the presence of our
Father, in the secret place, where our heart is encountered.
Those pursuing an Audience of One lifestyle find satisfaction in
the Lord's presence.

We may not see it in a day, a week or even a year, but the
pleasures found in the secret place are like unearthing a precious

stone. It might be covered by dirt and rock, but if we spend time chipping away at it, it will begin to reveal itself as the beautiful treasure it is.

We will begin to develop techniques and posture ourselves in a way that help make it easier and more effective to receive revelation of Him. Once in a while we will catch a glimpse of what's underneath the dirt and debris, and our spirit will energize. Often it's just enough to keep us going and push even harder, and the moments will strengthen our resolve for another extended length of time. The more we chip away, the more of these moments we will find. In time we will end up with something more precious than what we could ever have imagined.

God, reveal to me the treasures of being before You. I long
to spend my days gazing upon the beauty of my King and
uncovering layer after layer of who You are. Make me a person
who mines the mountain of Your heart and
uncovers the treasures of You.

We slander God by our very eagerness to work for Him without knowing Him.

-Oswald Chambers

SEVEN

SABBATICALS & BETTER CHOICES

Whether we enjoy our jobs and assignments on this earth or not, we all want to believe they are for a higher purpose, that they have meaning and impact. From the most mundane to the most stimulating assignments, God has made a way for us to find purpose and joy in them. We can set ourselves before the eyes of a living King and God no matter what we are doing.

Throughout history, the highest attainable assignment has always been to perform for royalty or to be in the king's service. Our king just happens to be God, the creator of heaven and earth.

Unlike the kings of old, God is not watching and waiting for us to mess up or make mistakes. He is not a tyrant who imposes his brutal will upon us. He is not like the bored kings of old who would say, "Off with your head!" simply for their amusement. He is a good king who rules in perfection and love. He has no character flaws, and He is always perfectly executing justice and love simultaneously. He observes all our activity with delight, just as a father watches his children at play.

LIKE A CHILD

When my children discover a new talent or master something that they haven't been able to do previously, they will come to me excitedly and ask me to watch what they are doing. It's been a few years since my seven year old discovered it, but it still makes me laugh and smile when he spins his arm super fast like a windmill. I remember when he first started doing this, he thought it was one of the most difficult tasks for the average person to perform. When he was in first grade, my wife and I had to lovingly convince him that it might not be the best idea to do this at the school talent show.

My kids don't come to me and expect me to criticize their new discoveries. They don't expect to be punished when they try something new and mess up. They don't expect me to chastise them for bothering me. They expect me to give them my full attention. Sometimes when they know I'm distracted, they place their little hands on both my cheeks and turn my face in the direction they want me to look. Since this actually works, why wouldn't they do it? When they have my attention, they seek my praise for their accomplishment no matter how small the accomplishment may be. They expect to hear words of affirmation, to see astonishment in my facial expression, and to know that I am proud of them.

If an imperfect, loving father like me can respond to his children this way, how much more can the perfect, loving Father God show interest and delight in His children? He is not removed from the heart of a father; He defines the heart of a father. He sets the bar.

We can find great joy in understanding that our Audience of One is also our Father. He longs for us to approach Him as children, and He longs to relate to us as a father. The same way the Father loves Jesus is the same way Jesus loves us.

No matter what age we are, if we had a father in our life, many of us can recall times when he either attended or missed an event we were involved in. Why is this so ingrained in our memories? What is it about the father's presence and approval that affects us so much? Even if there were hundreds of people at the event who enjoyed our performance, if our dad didn't show up, it didn't matter who else was there.

The absence of a father has a deep and lasting impact on a child, but our Father God has our constant attention and attendance. He never misses anything. Our Audience of One is always present and is waiting for us to delight Him.

God is jealous for the time that He gets to spend with His kids, and He wants to be the only one in the audience. He eagerly waits for us to marvel at our latest discoveries about Him. He wants us to rearrange our lives so that we simply come before Him and begin to relate to Him as our Father, and He will relate to us as His children.

Every little glance, every decision in life is important to God. The moments that we posture ourselves to give Him our love, attention and affection, and to ascribe to Him the glory due His name, matter on this side of eternity. He is a God who looks at the intentions of our hearts. He is eager to celebrate and display His pleasure over our small glances in His direction.

Our hearts are like a treasure box. When we give God our hearts in the secret place, we are making an eternal investment. He remembers the moments we choose to sit at His feet.

AT JESUS' FEET

This reminds me of two stories in Scripture about being at Jesus' feet. First, we have the story of "the sinful woman." She heard that Jesus was in the house of Simon the Pharisee. I find it interesting that she was able to get into the house to begin with. Who let her in? Who invited her? It is reminiscent of a verse in 1 Samuel:

> *He raises the poor from the dust*
> *And lifts the beggar from the ash heap,*
> *To set them among princes*
> *And make them inherit the throne of glory.*
> *"For the pillars of the earth are the Lord's,*
> *And He has set the world upon them."*

1 Samuel 2:8

This lowly woman, a sinner from the dust, found herself seated at the feet of Jesus, the Prince of Peace, and He honoured her. She proceeded to wash Jesus' feet with her tears and wipe them with her hair. Then she pulled out an alabaster jar of perfume to pour on His feet. Simon, the owner of the house, watched with disdain.

> *Now when the Pharisee who had invited Him saw this,*
> *he spoke to himself, saying, "This Man, if He were a*

prophet, would know who and what manner of woman
this is who is touching Him, for she is a sinner."

-Luke 7:39

Jesus had a response to Simon's accusation:

Then He turned to the woman and said to Simon, "Do
you see this woman? I entered your house; you gave Me
no water for My feet, but she has washed My feet with
her tears and wiped them with the hair of her head. You
gave Me no kiss, but this woman has not ceased to kiss My
feet since the time I came in. You did not anoint My head
with oil, but this woman has anointed
My feet with fragrant oil.

Therefore I say to you, her sins, which are many, are
forgiven, for she loved much. But to whom little is
forgiven, the same loves little."

-Luke 7:44-47

Simon had immediately disqualified Jesus' prophetic ministry
because Jesus allowed a well known sinner to touch Him and to
pour out her love at his feet. In chapter two, I talked about how
God validated Jesus' ministry when He sent His Spirit in the
form of a dove. Simon is doing the opposite here by despising
Jesus' ministry. He preferred to follow cultural and religious
traditions and judge accordingly. He allowed himself to be ruled
by a religious spirit and failed to recognize the One who sat
before him.

This woman came as she was and with all that she had. She didn't
have water to wash Jesus' feet; she had her tears. She didn't have
a towel to dry Jesus' feet; she had her hair. She had a costly jar of
perfume. She gave all that she had just to pour out her love on
Jesus' feet. What a beautiful picture!

Second and only a few chapters later, we find the story of Mary and Martha:

Now it happened as they went that He entered a certain village; and a certain woman named Martha welcomed Him into her house. And she had a sister called Mary, who also sat at Jesus' feet and heard His word. But Martha was distracted with much serving, and she approached Him and said, "Lord, do You not care that my sister has left me to serve alone? Therefore tell her to help me."

And Jesus answered and said to her, "Martha, Martha, you are worried and troubled about many things. But one thing is needed, and Mary has chosen that good part, which will not be taken away from her."

-Luke 10:38-42

Again we have a story of Jesus visiting a home. Martha probably had an idea of what she wanted her home to look like for Him. She spent time and energy preparing and making sure that everything was in order. Again we see a woman at Jesus' feet. Mary is sitting there while Martha is disdainfully observing her.

Jesus responds similarly to Martha as He did to Simon in the previous story. He tells Martha she is missing the whole point. He tells her only one thing is needed and that Mary has chosen the better thing. Martha spent more time on the structures around her to host Jesus than she did on her heart posture to respond to Him.

Both the sinful woman and Mary recognized the opportunity and who sat before them. Jesus validated their responses of sitting at His feet.

This is the posture of people who understand the Audience of One paradigm. They recognize this is where Jesus wants them—at His feet—and it is the only thing that is needed. In that place they gain revelation of Jesus' heart. They come as children not expecting to be condemned but approved.

SABBATICAL

During the time my parents were on a sabbatical from pastoring, a gentleman from the church our family was attending approached them after a service. This man had a strong prophetic gifting and was well respected in the church community. He told them, "I have a prophetic word for your son," so they called me over from my conversation with some of the young people.

He gave me a prophecy about what the Lord desired to do in my life regarding worship. Then he started prophesying to my parents. Although they had only just met him, he basically told them their life story and journey in ministry. He continued on to tell them that the next two years would be the most powerful years in their ministry. Now, my parents have had some good years in their service to the Lord. They had already seen a lot of healing, salvation, restoration and deliverance through their ministry. So when they heard this word, they were quite excited.

The two years passed quickly, and my parents remained on sabbatical. During this time they simply attended the church. They were really impacted by the worship, but they did little ministry. They saw minimal healing, salvation, restoration and deliverance, certainly not enough to justify the prophetic word they received. While those two years were good for their hearts, they did not see much impact their lives had on others. They considered going back into pastoral ministry, thinking that they should probably be a little more proactive.

However, at a church they often visited, one particular church member would walk up to them, look them in the eye and without knowing anything about the prophesy say, "Don't you do it. Don't even think about it!" This would happen whenever they needed to hear it.

After the two years, my dad evaluated things. He didn't get it; where was the power and impact? They hadn't ministered at all for the past two years let alone have a powerful ministry. He was confused and afraid that he might have missed it. He began crying out to God asking, "Lord, what's the deal? We haven't seen anything! You said these would be the most powerful years in our ministry."

My dad then got this response from the Lord: "Oh, but they have! You've spent the last two years where I wanted you all along—at My feet."

It was a defining moment for my parents, and the inspiring story of their journey would lead the way into my own discovery of choosing the better thing. Whenever I think of what the Lord spoke to my dad that day, it stirs my heart and solidifies the Audience of One call on my life.

Whenever I have those moments when I ask myself if I should be out there working for the Lord, I am always reminded that Jesus wants me at His feet. This is the most powerful ministry I can do. It's who I am and why He created me.

Being at His feet develops a burning heart. It's a heart that wants to bring others into the pleasure of being before God. It's a heart that wants to see the Great Commission fulfilled because it has seen the jealousy in Jesus' eyes for His bride.

God wants our ministry to be a result of sitting before Him first. The more time we spend with Him, the more we will be like Him and carry the same heart He has.

HOW JESUS FEELS

It's wonderful to grasp the importance of ministry to God. But if this is going to become a lifestyle and take root in our hearts, we have to know how Jesus feels about it and how He feels about us. With the two stories of the women at Jesus' feet, we can see His response and how He absolutely loved their heart posture. These simple acts of love and adoration recorded in His Holy Scripture will be remembered forever. It's astounding that something so simple and seemingly so ordinary as sitting at the feet of Jesus holds eternal significance.

When the sinful woman started weeping, what was it that caused her to do so? I don't think it was because she was grieving the loss of her wasted tears and precious perfume at his feet. I don't think it was that she looked at Jesus and saw He was angry, stoic, expressionless or unmoved by her actions. So what was it that made her weep?

This sinful woman sought out the Messiah and found Him. Her tears fell as she kissed His feet and as He announced her freedom from sin. She received revelation of a Messiah who accepted her in her lowly state and who with a heart full of mercy received her ministry unto Him. This is what we would call "the sure mercies of David" (Isaiah 55:3, Acts 13:34). In her brokenness, she didn't avoid Jesus; rather, she sought Him out and found mercy. She looked into Jesus' eyes and saw no condemnation, no indifference. When she looked at Jesus, He was moved and emanated mercy, love, joy and pleasure. I am confident she saw a giant smile.

We don't need to go much further than Song of Solomon to find out how the Lord feels about ministry to Him. The Shulamite sings the praises of the beloved and all His wonderful qualities. She is obsessed and enraptured with Him. What is the beloved's response to eyes that are looking at Him? He says:

> *You have ravished my heart,*
> *My sister, my spouse;*
> *You have ravished my heart*
> *With one look of your eyes,*
> *With one link of your necklace.*

-Song of Solomon 4:9

If this is the response to her small glance in His direction, how then does He feel about a life postured to be before His gaze? The revelation of this is staggering and should cause us to take our life and waste it on Him, to pour out our life and love at His feet.

The reality is that we don't stop to think about how He feels about our worship and small glances in His direction. How deeply is His heart connected with our response toward Him? When we go into the secret place to be with Him, do we understand how much it moves His heart? If we did I can guarantee that we'd be spending many more hours in the secret place. He desires us more than we desire Him, and that should cause true worship to arise from our hearts.

Lord, I thank you that You love my love. Thank You that I can approach You as a child sitting at Your feet. Help me to perpetually choose the better thing, so that I won't occupy myself with the things of life that take me away from sitting before You.

Whenever the method of worship becomes more important than the person of worship, we have already prostituted our worship. There are entire congregations who worship praise and praise worship but who have not yet learned to praise and worship God in Jesus Christ.

- Judson Cornwall

EIGHT

SUSTAINABLE MINISTRY & A BURNING HEART

Considering I'm someone who has always desired to be in ministry, it may come as a surprise to hear that I didn't always find it enjoyable. Rarely was it exciting, provoking, blissful or full of joy. I can recall multiple times having to lead youth group, worship or even play bass, where I did not look forward to it but even dreaded it. I felt like it was choking the life out of me. This always put me in a dilemma. I asked myself time after time why I wanted to be in ministry so badly if I didn't actually enjoy it.

While I know I had good intentions and I was sincere in my love for God, the simple fact remained that I wasn't ministering to bring glory to God or to please Him. I was ministering to share my gifting, to enhance the Christian experience in others and to build my influence in ministry.

One evening I was street preaching with the Midnight Martyrs at the university campus. We chose the lobby outside of a gym during a basketball game to do our evangelism, and the group decided on a question to approach people with in order to engage them in a conversation about God. Since we didn't want to bombard people as a group and scare them away, we took turns doing one on one conversations.

It was my turn to go after watching a few do it with some level of success. I looked around the lobby and found the least threatening person I could find: a man in his mid to late fifties, kind looking with a salt and pepper beard and glasses. I nervously approached him with the question we had decided on: "Good evening, Sir. My friends and I are interviewing random people around the campus. Do you mind if I take a minute of your time and ask you a question?"

"Sure," he replied.

I asked, "What comes to your mind when you hear the word *God*?"

And out of his mouth came: "It depends what you mean about God. Do you blah, blah, blah, . . ."

It was like I was a child listening to a grownup in a Charlie Brown cartoon. When he finished, I simply replied, "Thank you for your time," and turned and walked quickly in the opposite direction. One of the guys in our group, who went to the university, laughed and told me, "You chose to ask the question to a world religions professor!"

I felt inadequate. I possessed a lot of zeal and love but little revelation on the God I was trying to convey to people. This gave me profound respect for evangelists and people with the ability to share the gospel with others so effectively. I believe it's something we all need to learn to do in our various walks of life, and it's a good reminder of how much we need to know God.

You can love God and have great zeal for others to be saved, but if you don't know who He is, it's like trying to convince people how awesome a certain food is, even though you have not actually tried it yourself.

My friend Tyler from Midnight Martyrs was asked to preach and lead worship at a three-day long camp just outside the city, and I was invited to come and play bass. Most of the kids at the camp were about the same age as me, so it felt a bit strange to be on stage leading them. The worship and the speaking went quite late one evening, and there was a group of about four kids who did not respond to anything. They sat clumped together in the corner of the chapel, dressed in black and wearing band t-shirts. They didn't sing, wouldn't come up for altar calls or even smile. They looked completely bored and grouchy. This bothered me because I knew that they were missing out on what God was doing with the rest of the kids at camp.

After the second night, Tyler came up to me and asked, "How would you feel about preaching at the chapel service tomorrow morning?"

I was surprised by the question and it made me a little nervous, but by this time I'd preached enough off-the-cuff sermons that I knew I could put something together quickly. Since it was a morning session and a little more laid back, I agreed. I thought I had a message to preach that would get those four young people to respond.

I went home that night and wrote my sermon. I remembered that this was going to be the third service since the camp began and, therefore, the third opportunity for these young people to respond to an altar call. My message ended up being about Peter denying Jesus three times.

I don't remember the whole message, but when I came to the end of my sermon, I looked in the general direction of the foursome, and with as much authority as I could muster up, I said, "We had three worship times this weekend, three opportunities to respond to Jesus, and some of us have denied Jesus all three times."

Looking back, I realize now how horribly wrong it was of me to try to guilt trip people into responding to worship and the salvation message. Needless to say, the altar call response was light. Hoping to be rescued from this weak ministry time, I quickly asked the worship leader to go into another song.

I fell flat on my face delivering that message, but why? I concluded that I didn't try to bring glory to Jesus; instead, I tried to cause a response in people. I should have just declared who Jesus is and let fascination for an amazing man take over. I didn't speak about God; I tried to preach a message about one man's weakness and how we should not be like him by making the same mistake. Not only was the message wrong in its theology, but it didn't produce anything positive either.

The Lord quickly corrected me, and I heard Him simply say, "Okay, now it's time to make it about Me."

There are countless times that I've made mistakes like this. The Lord, full of grace and love, enjoys us even in our immaturity and growing pains. Sometimes He will even surprise us and do a good work in the midst of our struggles and mistakes. I had good intentions about making a difference in people's hearts, but I was misguided and delivered the message poorly. I didn't see the bigger picture that God wants to touch people's hearts, and all He wants me to do is direct attention to Him.

I wasn't serving out of the understanding that when I minister, it is before Him only. I'm not the first one to preach a sermon that was directed to specific people. Some build a ministry doing it, and that's when a preacher can become weak. You could last three, five, even ten years in your own strength in ministry, but what's the point if you end up burned out and disillusioned in your walk with God?

It happens with leaders and pastors time and time again. They go about working in their own strength with integrity and good intentions, but they miss out on ministering to the Lord. They try to improve the human condition by ministering to people rather than to God. There is nothing wrong with directing a message to people, but it should be through the Lord's direction and heart for them.

How does He feel? What is He speaking? The Lord is the one who is ultimately going to impact others through us. He wants a partnership.

I have often gotten into arguments with others who quote certain Scripture to emphasize ministry to people. Take this passage, for example:

"'for I was hungry and you gave Me food; I was thirsty and you gave Me drink; I was a stranger and you took Me in; I was naked and you clothed Me; I was sick and you visited Me; I was in prison and you came to Me.'"

"Then the righteous will answer Him, saying, 'Lord, when did we see You hungry and feed You, or thirsty and give You drink? When did we see You a stranger and take You in, or naked and clothe You? Or when did we see You sick, or in prison, and come to You?' And the King will answer and say to them, 'Assuredly, I say to you, inasmuch as you did it to one of the least of these My brethren, you did it to Me.'"

-Matthew 25:35-40

I love this passage because it reveals the heart of Jesus for people and how He wants us to partner with Him in loving His bride, the church. Contrary to what some may think, it does not devalue the Audience of One message. It actually gives it more emphasis.

This goes along the same lines as Jesus' two commandments. The first is the greatest (loving God), but the second is like it (loving people). The key part that can be missed in this passage is that Jesus made sure to include Himself in this teaching. Helping people in need was not about ministering to people, but ministering to the Lord. He wanted His audience to know that when they fed the hungry, visited prisoners and cared for the sick that they were doing it for Him. Jesus said it in a way that was meant to be the motivation for us when we minister: "You did it for Me."

What happens when we acquire the Lord's heart in bringing Him all the glory and ministering unto Him? It results in the

Lord's heart for humanity being poured out on us. If you want to have an effective ministry, minister to the Lord's heart first, and then watch Him move through you. Watch how it will be so much more effective and life-giving to you in the process.

LONGINGS OF THE HEART

The Lord puts longings into every human being. These longings are designed to fulfil our purpose in bringing Him pleasure in whatever assignment we have. We often feel the ache of these longings and think we will satisfy it by focusing on the assignment God has for us. That focus often looks like working for Him, doing something tangible to further His purposes.

We need to understand that the ache is simply a priestly longing, the Holy Spirit at work inside of us desiring to glorify the Son and to minister to Jesus.

The question is, what ministry matters in heaven? Evangelists, healers, preachers and pastors will not be needed in heaven. While these are all necessary now, if they are the essence of our identity and how we define our ministries, how are we going to define our existence in heaven?

What is the one ministry that will not stop when our lives on this side of heaven come to an end? It is ministry to God. Worship and adoration of the King, ministry to the Audience of One, will never stop. What can we do now that will continue in heaven and make our ministry on earth more powerful?

The moment our activity ceases to be about us or others is the moment we can begin to bring glory to Jesus in that activity. It is the moment we can begin to move forward into our destiny. He must be the focus.

To sustain a lifestyle of ministry to Jesus, we need a revelation that this is our destiny in this age as well as in the age to come. We should not separate our destiny in heaven from how we live on earth. If Jesus is going to be the centre of our ministry and the object of our gaze forever, then this needs to be the posture we take now.

Therefore we make it our aim, whether present or absent, to be well pleasing to Him.

-2 Corinthians 5:9

Many spend their efforts building their ministry through establishing bigger churches, attracting more people and gaining more influence. But if we look at Jesus, He did things differently. He often tried to get away from the crowds. He wanted to find a quiet place of solitude where He could spend time with God in prayer and worship.

Then we come to the moment in Luke 22 when Jesus actually wants His company to pray with Him and sit before God alongside Him. And what happens? They all fall asleep! It was easy for the disciples to get excited about being with Jesus when they saw miracles and when He was providing for their needs, teaching and taking them places. But when it came time to sit with Him and pray to the Father, they grew weary. This was right before the greatest moment in history, when Jesus takes on death!

To live the Audience of One lifestyle, God needs to be the centre of it all, when things look bright in ministry as well as in the times when the lights are out. He wants us to tarry with Him. He enjoys our company, and it's His pleasure for us to be by His side. However, do we grow weary and sleep in those moments when He asks, "Will you stay with me?"

WILL THE REAL PETER STEP UP?

After preaching my failed sermon, I came to understand the story of Peter in a different light. It turns out that it is a lot more fascinating than what I had presented to those young people.

If you know the story of Peter, you know that during the last supper Jesus told Peter that he would deny Him three times. Peter goes on to do exactly that.

How is it that despite all that Peter saw and witnessed while walking with God in the flesh, he was still weak enough to deny Jesus? It is so easy to judge Peter, yet we have the benefit of the Holy Spirit living within us and often ignore His presence.

However, there is an interesting story of redemption for Peter in John 21 that absolutely has to do with ministering out of an Audience of One paradigm. Jesus rose from the dead and began appearing to His disciples. Before Peter had denied Him, Jesus had already told Peter that his future ministry would be to build His church (Matthew 16:18). In John 21, Jesus reveals how Peter is to do this ministry:

> *So when they had eaten breakfast, Jesus said to Simon Peter, "Simon, son of Jonah, do you love Me more than these?"*
> *He said to Him, "Yes, Lord; You know that I love You."*
> *He said to him, "Feed My lambs."*
> *He said to him again a second time, "Simon, son of Jonah, do you love Me?"*
> *He said to Him, "Yes, Lord; You know that I love You."*
> *He said to him, "Tend My sheep."*
> *He said to him the third time, "Simon, son of Jonah, do you love Me?" Peter was grieved because He said to him the third time, "Do you love Me?"*

And he said to Him, "Lord, You know all things; You know that I love You."
Jesus said to him, "Feed My sheep."

-John 21:15-17

Redemption came after Peter denied Jesus three times. Jesus brought healing to Peter's heart by re-affirming Peter's love for Him three times. I believe Peter needed this encouragement to be able to shepherd the sheep that Jesus was talking about.

In each of the three statements in the John 21 passage, the phrase referring to the sheep (or the ministry of the church) varied. But the one constant through all three statements was Jesus' question, "Do you love me?"

No matter what Peter's ministry looked like, Jesus wanted Peter's love first. He desired Peter's ministry to be fuelled by love and by a revelation of Himself.

Love and devotion to Jesus is paramount in order for Jesus to be our only audience and for Him to receive the praise of His glory from the human heart. Are we willing to put in the time to find out who He is? Are we willing to let our eyes be captivated by the most fascinating man ever to walk this earth? Is our ministry and life's work going to be fuelled by our love for Him?

Attending Sunday worship and slipping back into life's routines for the rest of the week is not enough. Doing a 15 minute devotional in the morning and then getting down to business won't cut it either. No matter where we think we are in our walk with God, we always need to make Him the focus of our attention as our starting point. There are depths of love that we will be forever uncovering, and we are missing out if we are not perpetually seeking them out.

As the Father loved Me, I also have loved you;
abide in My love.

-John 15:9

Remaining or abiding in His love is not an intermittent experience; it's a continuous and all-consuming one. If Jesus loves us the same way that the Father loves Him, it means He wants to relate to us the same way that He does with the Father. What does this look like? While on earth He only did what He saw the Father doing and said what He heard the Father saying. In this lifetime we will not attain to the level of unity Jesus has with the Father, but we now have a path forward into what He desires.

One of my favourite quotes from A.W. Tozer is, "We are called to an everlasting preoccupation with God." How consuming is this preoccupation? I like how Peter described it:

If anyone speaks, let him speak as the oracles of God. If
anyone ministers, let him do it as with the ability which
God supplies, that in all things God may be glorified
through Jesus Christ, to whom belong the glory and the
dominion forever and ever. Amen.

-1 Peter 4:11

How much glory we give Jesus is proportional to how worthy we think He is to receive it. While this is sobering, remember that the means of accomplishing it is through love, relationship and fascination. We can't abide in Him and love Him unless He helps us.

WHAT ABOUT CHRISTIAN ENTERTAINERS?

I have wrestled with this question for years. How can God be our Audience of One if our very job is to entertain people? There is a whole Christian entertainment industry including a large array of bands, writers, filmmakers, artists and even comedians. So where *do* they fit in this message?

I think it is a good idea to start by looking at the fruit they produce. Just as there are carpenters who produce furniture for people to enjoy, authors who write books for people to read, and gardeners who grow flowers to make things beautiful, God has given us songwriters and musicians to create music for us to enjoy and entertain us. Because what they do is so public, artists may have a stronger temptation to receive glory for themselves, but it is not for us to judge their heart intentions.

Christian artists need to search their own hearts and ask themselves if their ministry is for God's fame or theirs. They must evaluate and look at the fruit that is being produced by their own hearts.

A great prayer for those pursuing an Audience of One lifestyle is to pray, "Lord, search my heart," much like David prayed. Is our goal to make people love us more? Or do we focus on Jesus? Are we producing art with all our heart, soul and mind for the purposes of honouring God with the gifts He has given us?

I am convinced that Christian artists and entertainers are a gift to us from the Lord. What would we do without art that stirs our fascination toward God? What would we do without music and stories that touch our hearts and move our emotions?

The Lord has given Christian artists and entertainers these gifts to share with the Body of Christ. God loves all the arts. He is the great artist. We are free to enjoy them as long as it produces good fruit in us. But if enjoying a particular form of art hinders growth in our hearts and weakens our love for God, it might be a good idea to re-evaluate what we are enjoying.

Simply put, Christian artists need to entertain in a way that brings glory to God. Artists need to entertain in a way that establishes God as their only audience. It is a heart posture we are looking for.

No matter what we do, we should ask ourselves this simple question: Is my activity provoking God to jealousy for His glory and fame, or is it bringing Him glory and fame?

If we are living before God as our sole audience, we will no longer be living to please man, which always leads to dullness and boredom. We will be living to please God. The fuel we have been given to sustain our ministry to God, no matter what we do, is the fascination of His beauty and love. This produces people who long to bring Him all the glory.

> Lord, help me to love You more. Take me into the mystery of what You said when You declared to the Father that You love me the same way He loves You. I want to honour You with my eyes, my ears and my whole body, and with all my emotions and my activity. Produce good fruit in my heart and receive all the glory and fame in all that I do.

Lord, stamp eternity on my eyeballs.

-Jonathan Edwards

NINE

ETERNITY & NEXT STEPS

If the perfect reflection of the Audience of One paradigm is represented by the activity that surrounds God's throne in heaven, how should this affect our time and activity on the earth right now?

Humanity is experiencing an identity crisis. Godless men and women are constantly devising new ways to glorify humanity and convincing themselves that they can live righteously without God.

Secular science theory is attempting to steal God's glory revealed through creation. Meteorologists are ignoring the sovereignty of God's power over weather by attributing climate change and natural disasters to man's activity alone. The movie and entertainment industries are attempting to distract us by stealing our fascination with the beauty of God that we are destined to behold, and are substituting counterfeit pleasures. And the social justice movement outside of the church is wanting to make positive changes in people's lives and hearts apart from Jesus, which is fine in the short term, but is lacking God's grace and power to redeem lives for eternity.

Instead of turning their hearts to God in the midst of disasters, people rise up with the human spirit. I often hear people say in the midst of disaster and chaos that human pride will not be defeated. They say we will rise up again and will come out stronger than ever, when all along it was God's intention to save us from our pride, to bring us back into alignment with His kingdom, and to strengthen us in righteousness and holiness. There is a world movement that actively wars against God's right to receive glory and His sovereignty.

Though it seems now that very few people are giving themselves to the Audience of One lifestyle, there is good news. Jesus is the King, and He will return to the earth to establish His kingdom of priests. The same scientists, meteorologists, artists and humanitarians who glorify human achievement will bow before Jesus as King and confess that He is Lord.

Therefore God also has highly exalted Him and given Him the name which is above every name, that at the name of Jesus every knee should bow, of those in heaven, and of those on earth, and of those under the earth, and that every tongue should confess that Jesus Christ is Lord, to the glory of God the Father.

-Philippians 2:9-11

All the ends of the world
Shall remember and turn to the Lord,
And all the families of the nations
Shall worship before You.

-Psalm 22:27

God is not stoic and uninvolved with us and His creation. He intends to bring about a change. All the nations will come and worship Him whether it's in this age or the next. God fully intends to be glorified by every being. There will come a day when there will be widespread knowledge across the earth of the glory of God.

For the earth will be filled
With the knowledge of the glory of the Lord,
As the waters cover the sea.

-Habakkuk 2:14

All nations whom You have made
Shall come and worship before You, O Lord,
And shall glorify Your name.

-Psalm 86:9

While there is a day coming when God will have everyone's attention and worship, He is looking for our response right now. In the same psalm, David goes on to say:

I will praise You, O Lord my God, with all my heart,
And I will glorify Your name forevermore.

-Psalm 86:12

David understood that his primary calling in this age and the next was to bring glory to God. There is no higher calling. We want to be in full, voluntary agreement with God's call to worship before He returns, because when He does return, it will be involuntary.

People ministering to the Audience of One grasp God's supremacy. They know He formed their inward parts and has full authority over the intricacies of life. They know He is God of the big and small things. They know that He holds all things together and they exist for His pleasure. He puts breath in their lungs. They are confident in Him because they understand that all things exist for His glory.

> *He is the image of the invisible God, the firstborn over*
> *all creation. For by Him all things were created that are*
> *in heaven and that are on earth, visible and invisible,*
> *whether thrones or dominions or principalities or powers.*
> *All things were created through Him and for Him. And*
> *He is before all things, and in Him all things consist.*
> *And He is the head of the body, the church, who is the*
> *beginning, the firstborn from the dead, that in all things*
> *He may have the preeminence.*
>
> -Colossians 1:15-18

God will have supremacy in all things. I believe the greatest power to come in healing, salvation, revival and miracles will be out of this place of ministry and worship to God. He wants to make His name famous.

MINISTRY POWER THROUGH WORSHIP

In my late teens, I was in a Christian band. There were five of us from the same class at school. Our performances consisted of singing to soundtracks. We didn't play any instruments. I don't know how we managed to get gigs, but we lined up a few at youth groups, school and camps. People even called into the local Christian radio station asking to hear a song by our band. Of course, the DJ didn't know what people were talking about.

The Lord did some amazing things through us that year. The band members and our classmates saw a lot of healing. We prayed for each other all the time and witnessed things such as legs that grew in front of our eyes and broken bones that instantly healed.

One time I was playing basketball at an inter-Christian school basketball tournament. As I jumped for a layup, I fell sideways on my ankle and heard a snap. Our captain, who was also the lead singer in the band, quickly called a time-out and helped me limp off the court in great pain. The coach was about to send out someone in my place, but before the coach even got to look at my ankle, the captain gathered the team around me. They prayed for my ankle, and I stood up and went right back on the court for the next play. My ankle was healed.

It was all so seamless and seemed normal for us to walk in that kind of healing power from on high. There were many similar stories involving our little group.

There was one gig that sticks out in my memory. We were singing at a youth group one Friday night. We performed a couple of songs and then, in the midst of the worship time, one of our singers called up the youth for prayer. People came up to the stage, and we prayed for them. There were several people healed that night, including a deaf ear being opened! I believe this will be a regular occurrence in the years to come.

Increasingly, people are going to be touched by God in the midst of simply worshipping Him, not necessarily during an altar call, but just by a sovereign work of the Holy Spirit on hearts that are focused on Him. He is going to release power on people because their hearts are devoted to giving Him glory.

STADIUM FULL OF GLORY

When I was about 15, I had one of the most intense dreams of my entire life. In my dream, a packed stadium stretched before me. I had a bird's-eye view, looking out over the relatively quiet crowd of spectators.

I then found myself standing on the field. A band came onto the stage set up in the middle of the field and started to sing worship songs. It was obvious they were there to bring glory to Jesus, but the crowd seemed to be ignoring them entirely.

I was standing beside the stage when suddenly I started to shake under the power of God. I stepped onto the stage and walked to the microphone that the worship leader was using. In the middle of the song, I called everyone to repent and to turn to God. I felt a rumble under my feet. The whole stadium began to shake as in an earthquake. Everybody started shaking, and many fell on their faces, crying out to God in the midst of this worship time.

When I awoke from the dream, I was sweating and trembling. Although we were not living in a revival at that time, I got to experience one in my dream. It was a revival in my heart that happened in the midst of worship.

I truly believe we will see this dream fulfilled again and again in the days ahead. God will bring salvation and repentance in the midst of people who are simply singing praises to Him.

The stadium was full of the glory of God, and I can't wait to see what it will look like when the whole earth is full of His glory! No longer will we see revivals fizzle out because an individual becomes the centre of attention. We will witness a move of God that will have a lasting impact because God is taking centre stage. It all culminates with Him returning to the earth to establish a kingdom of worshippers.

STAMP ETERNITY ON OUR EYEBALLS

There is a mindset dominating a lot of the church that says the things of eternity and heaven are too confusing, so we need not focus on them. The very fact that many people find these things confusing should be reason enough to spend our time finding out as much as we can about them. Heaven is where we are going to live one day, not for the mere 70 to 100 years that we have in this age, but forever.

If we truly believe Jesus' prayer for God's kingdom to be established on earth as it is in heaven, we need to understand what it is like in heaven and come into agreement with it. The Audience of One paradigm hinges upon what we think of heaven. If this does not ring true for us, what else do we think we will be doing there? Everything in heaven is centred around God's throne. All eyes are on Him, and His glory is everywhere. The best thing about heaven is that we get to look upon Jesus' physical frame and see Him with our unveiled eyes.

Many people think that they should just make the best of this life and let heaven take care of itself. It's somewhat true that we need to be earthly-minded in this age, but even better is the culture of heaven imposing itself on the earth. Jesus understood this when He told us to pray for His kingdom to be established on earth as it is in heaven. He truly wants us to enjoy life in this age now, but He desires that we would would look to eternity in determining how we live.

> *But store up for yourselves treasures **in heaven**, where moths and vermin do not destroy, and where thieves do not break in and steal. **For where your treasure is, there your heart will be also.***

-Matthew 6:20,21
(emphasis mine)

God wants our hearts and longings set on eternity, on the things of heaven where He is the only audience. God placed this yearning in all of our hearts as a gift to sustain our worship and our hope.

> *For in this we groan, earnestly desiring to be clothed with our habitation which is from heaven.*

-2 Corinthians 5:2

FINDING MY WAY INTO MINISTRY

I came across Amos 5:4 in my teens at a time in my life when I was defining my walk with God. I asked the Lord for a Scripture to lean on and remember, in whatever life situation I found myself, so that I could keep my foundation firm and my ministry focused. I opened my Bible one day and Amos 5:4 leaped out to me.

> *Seek me and live;*

-Amos 5:4b

Instantly I knew and I said excitedly, "I found it! This is my verse!" Year after year it has continued to make a mark on my heart and has kept me in the place of seeking the Lord first above all else. This verse has been crucial to me in living out the Audience of One lifestyle.

THE HOUSE OF PRAYER

It has always been on my heart to do full time ministry in the area of worship. It was just a question of what it was going to look like and when it was going to happen. In 2005, God began moving my wife's heart and my heart to transition into something new, although we were not entirely sure what it was going to be.

It quickly became evident that God was going to build a house of prayer in Winnipeg, and we would be part of the team to help establish it. This prompted a trip to the house of prayer in Kansas City where 24-hour worship and prayer had already been in place for several years.

I went with a group that was interested in the house of prayer and wanted to know more about it. Some friends who made the trip previously told me how they were blown away by what they encountered in the place of sustained worship and prayer. Still, I was unsure what to expect or how I would respond.

It was a long, 14-hour drive south from Winnipeg to Kansas City. As soon as we arrived, we headed straight to the prayer room. The second I walked in, I smelled the fragrance of worship. It felt easy to worship in that environment. As I read the Bible, every word came alive.

I thought to myself, *Of course there is day and night worship and prayer! Why wouldn't there be? I was made for this.* It felt like I was returning home after many years on a long journey.

Eventually we made the transition to help establish the house of prayer in Winnipeg. Fast forward from 2005 to the present and we now find ourselves rooted in a community that is built for the Audience of One lifestyle. It is a place to come and gaze upon the Lord together.

Over the years the Lord had been preparing me for this. It was not until eight years later while serving in the house of prayer that the Lord encountered me in a significant way during a trip to that same Kansas City prayer room. He nudged me to leave my job working in a public school. He wanted me to spend my days living before Him in ministry as what is formally known as an intercessory missionary.

However, I prefer to describe it as being a priest. Doing this full-time is not for everyone, but we can all find a way to be before the Lord as the Audience of One and do everything for His glory in whatever our occupation or ministry. We have all been invited to find our prayer closets. We can all gain eternal perspectives and bring God pleasure and give Him glory. Each and every one of us will find joy and fulfilment when we place ourselves before the Audience of One.

Once we have an encounter with God, we should automatically be drawn to see the beauty of His holiness. This was what Moses wanted when he encountered the Lord, to see His beauty and His face.

And he [Moses] said, "Please, show me your glory."

-Exodus 33:18

Life takes on meaning when we set our eyes on God alone. What will we see when we fix our eyes on God? We will see eyes of fire that are fixed on us. What is His face expressing as we live before

Him? It is expressing divine pleasure. What does His smile look like? It looks like the broad smile of a loving Father delighted by His children. And that makes living out an Audience of One lifestyle worth it all.

Lord, stamp eternity on my eyeballs! Let it be on earth as it is in heaven where You are the centre of it all. Make ministry to Your heart my first place. Open up my eyes to see more beauty, majesty and glory. Let incense arise from my heart. Hour by hour, day by day, cause Your glory to be manifested in me.

ABOUT THE AUTHOR

Johan serves on staff as an intercessory missionary at Sanctuary House of Prayer Missions Base in Winnipeg, Manitoba, Canada, where he lives with his wife, Corrie, and three children, Eli, Caitlin and Luke. In addition to his ministry as an intercessory missionary, Johan is a worship leader and songwriter. He often serves in various church communities to encourage and strengthen them in the "Audience of One" message.

To learn more, or to contact Johan, visit his website at:
www.johanheinrichs.com

CPSIA information can be obtained at www.ICGtesting.com
Printed in the USA
LVOW12s0736290414

383584LV00008B/21/P